Date Due

OCT 30			
NOV 1 2			
NOV 2 6			
JAN 2 3			
FEB 17			
APR 11			
MAR 1 2			
	PRINTED	IN U. S. A.	

THE THREE STAGES OF

THE SPIRITUAL LIFE

THE THREE STAGES OF
The Spiritual Life
Under the Inspiration of Jesus

By J. GRIMAL, S.M., S.T.D.

Translated Into English Under the Direction of
JOSEPH BUCKLEY, S.M.

VOLUME I

First Stage of the Spiritual Life

TRUE CONVERSION OF HEART

THE BRUCE PUBLISHING COMPANY
MILWAUKEE

Rosary College Dewey Classification Number: 248

Library of Congress Catalog Card Number: 56-7737

© 1956 by The Bruce Publishing Company
MADE IN THE UNITED STATES OF AMERICA

Translator's Preface

FATHER JULES GRIMAL died, August 31, 1953, in Belley, France. His memory will remain a warm and gentle inspiration to those who learned from his words and the example of his life how to live for God. The sincerity with which he endeavored to live that complete dedication to Jesus he taught to others was remarkable. His solution to many problems was "Try to forget yourself and think of Jesus." One could see and sense that Father Grimal did at all times forget Father Grimal and think of Christ. Father Grimal was ever understanding, reasonable, moderate. Other superiors might say, "You have the reasons but I have the authority." Not Father Grimal. He preferred to let himself be imposed upon rather than to brush aside the reasons advanced by those who came to him for permission or assistance.

This translation of Father Grimal's three little French volumes on the stages of the spiritual life is meant, therefore, as a testimony of affection for the man as well as of admiration for his writing. It is a matter of deep regret to the translator that the publication in English of this work of Father Grimal did not take place in Father Grimal's lifetime. He desired it so much. After all, he had spent twenty devoted and fruitful years in the United States as teacher of theology[1] and master of the spiritual life,[2] so that when he left to become a member of the General Administration of the

---

[1] Father Grimal taught theology at Marist College, Washington, D. C., from 1903 to 1914. During the last six years of this period, he was also superior of this major seminary of the Marist Fathers.

[2] Father Grimal was master of novices during practically the whole period 1914 to 1923, directing either the first or second (tertianship) novitiates of the Marist Fathers.

Society of Mary, in Rome,[3] he took with him special concern for his spiritual sons and daughters in the United States.[4] Father Grimal felt that by his works translated into English[5] he continued, although absent in person, his maturing influence on the supernatural life of the growing Marist family and of all their associates, clerical, religious, and lay, in English-speaking countries.

The publication in English of the present work, delayed as it has been by a wartime army chaplaincy, a pastorate, and various intervening obligations, would, in all likelihood, not even now be achieved were it not for the valuable assistance of Father George Bracho, S.M., in the translation of the first two volumes. I am grateful to Father Joseph C. Jaubert for his painstaking check and completion of references. To Father John McQuade, S.M., I am indebted for generous research and wise counsel with regard to Father Grimal's opinion that the sacramental character of baptism is the formal cause in Christians of their share in Jesus' divine sonship, as it is indeed of their association in His priesthood. Sanctifying grace, in this view, would simply make us *worthy* sons of God. After careful consideration, it has seemed prudent to eliminate this singular opinion and to edit Father Grimal's work, especially

---

[3] When Father Grimal first joined the General Administration in 1923, it was located at Moncalieri, near Turin. In 1925 he moved with it to Rome. During World War II, Father Grimal with the rest of the General Administration spent two years, 1940–42, at La Neyliere, near Lyons, France, and then returned to Rome. Father Grimal was assistant to the Superior General from 1923 to 1947 and also Marist Procurator to the Holy See from 1928 to 1947.

[4] Father Grimal was an excellent retreat master for Sisters and helped the Missionary Sisters of the Society of Mary and other communities in the composition or editing of their constitutions.

[5] *The Priesthood and Sacrifice of Our Lord Jesus Christ,* translated by His Excellency, the Most Reverend Michael Keyes, S.M. (Philadelphia: McVey, 1915). *With Jesus to the Priesthood,* translated by His Excellency, the Most Reverend Gerald Shaughnessy, S.M. (Philadelphia: The Dolphin Press, 1932). *To Die With Jesus,* translated by Bishop Shaughnessy (New York: The Macmillan Company, 1925).

the third volume, in favor of the accepted doctrine that sancti-
fying grace itself is the formal cause that makes us children of
God. This alteration does not at all affect the substance of
Father Grimal's work.

Let it be said at this point that there are other opinions
expressed in this work in which the present translator does
not entirely concur. Such differences of opinion are to be
expected. They do not affect the substance of Father Grimal's
exposition of the supernatural life. It has not seemed to me
that I should tamper with Father Grimal's statement of his
views. Only in one case have I indicated in a footnote that
I do not consider solid the author's opinion that those who
make public temporary vows undertake thereby a sort of
obligation to remain permanently in the religious life.

While Father Grimal's activities and contacts were in large
measure with priests, students for the priesthood, and religious
and his examples are most frequently chosen from their life
and problems, it would be an unfortunate mistake to think
that this work is of interest and value only for them. Many
earnest laypeople will find here just the explanations and
illuminations they have been seeking to make their spiritual
life more meaningful and to dispel doubts which have dis-
turbed them. When, here and there, they encounter a chapter
which seems to them over-technical, they have only to pass
over it lightly to discover in the very next chapter words
that will appear indeed to come from the heart of Christ
Himself. Father Grimal in this outline of the supernatural
life keeps close to the Gospels and is eminently psychological
and practical.

May we ask that those who find Father Grimal's work a
help in drawing closer to the Lord, remember kindly in their
prayers the author, the translators, and the patient publisher.

St. Pius X Parish, Bedford, Ohio
Thanksgiving Day, 1955

Author's Foreword

WHEN in 1935 the editor of the *Cahiers Thomistes* requested that I contribute some articles of a theological character on Christian spirituality, I went first and as by instinct to the subject that attracts every Christian soul: the filial life of Jesus in Himself and in us. The following year, these articles were published together in a volume with the title, taken from the Epistle to the Galatians:[1] *It Is Christ That Lives in Me*. In 1937, when a request was made that I resume the composition of articles for the *Cahiers,* I turned back, as it were, and wrote a series of essays on *True Conversion of Heart* and *True Work of Progress*. These were republished simultaneously at the beginning of 1940 in two volumes as a study of the first two stages of the spiritual life. Since then, I let myself be convinced by friendly, authoritative representations that with one modification in the title, several slight changes in the text, and an introduction on the filial character of our union of love with the Father, the volume which had appeared four years before could take its place after the two others as their natural culmination.

This logical arrangement of the treatises was first made in an Italian translation published at the beginning of 1944 by the *Opera di San Paolo* and the three attractive little volumes give indeed the impression of a single work on the three stages of the spiritual life. Now, thanks be to God, I find it possible to make this same change in a new French edition. The *It Is Christ That Lives in Me* of 1935 will take its proper place in the series under this new title *Third Stage*

---

[1] 2:20.

*of the Spiritual Life Under the Inspiration of Jesus — The
True Life of Union With the Father.*

Although the position and title of this volume are changed,
there is no modification in its object or aim. It still does not
seek to propound the intimate nature of mystical union with
God. To me it would seem rash to attempt, without personal
experience, without special initiation, to treat of the essence
and degrees of a life that is dominated by the profoundly
mysterious action proper to the Holy Spirit, on the threshold
of which the great masters of the spiritual life and the saints
themselves hesitate and find themselves at variance.

Just as the first two volumes seek to emphasize above all
else the role of Christ the Saviour in the work of Conversion
and Progress, so the third volume aims to describe the supreme
culmination of this work as our participation in the life of
filial love of Jesus for the Father. This goal is not outside
the compass of anyone who, with the aid of Catholic com-
mentaries, studies and meditates the New Testament. It has
pleased the Holy Spirit to reveal there the filial life of our
Saviour in His own heart and to cause us to hear His in-
vitations to communicate in this life, especially in the Gospel
of St. John, the Gospel of "Jesus Christ, life and the author
of life," as Father Lagrange has described it.[2]

It is thus "under the inspiration of Jesus" that the three
volumes, like the three stages of the spiritual life which they
describe, find unity and completeness. Perhaps the constant
reminder of this presence and this action of Christ Jesus
throughout the whole conduct of our life in God constitutes
the sole originality of these studies in spiritual theology, if
originality they do possess. May they assist us to an ever fuller
recognition of the necessary presence of Christ in our whole
journey toward perfection, from the first steps on the way of

[2] M. J. Lagrange, O.P., *Evangile selon S. Jean* (Paris: Gabalda, 1927), clxiii.

conversion to the very summits of the union of love. Above all, may these studies induce us to surrender ourselves with our whole heart to the action of Him who is "the way, the truth, and the life"; without whom "nobody can come to the Father."[3]

Feast of the Annunciation, 1945
Rome

---

[3] Jn. 14:6.

Contents

THE THREE STAGES OF

THE SPIRITUAL LIFE

Introduction ✤ Nature and Degrees of Perfection

I. Nature of Perfection

THE perfection of a being consists in general in the acquisition and possession of all the elements which are proper to its nature. Ordinarily speaking, something is called perfect when it is "completed," "finished," according to its proper character, a being which lacks nothing of what it should possess: "that to which nothing is wanting."[1]

A being stops, so to speak, once it reaches perfection; it has attained its goal, its end. If it is capable of understanding the fullness of this goodness, it rejoices in it and is happy; for joy or happiness is the sign that an existence has succeeded, that a being has reached its destiny.

> Philosophers who have speculated on the meaning of life and on the destiny of man have not given adequate attention to the fact that nature takes care to instruct us on this point. She informs us by a precise sign when destiny is attained. This sign is joy. I say *joy,* and not pleasure. Pleasure is merely an artifice invented by nature to obtain from the living being the conservation of life; it does not indicate the direction toward which life tends. Joy, on the other hand, always announces that life has succeeded, that it has gained ground, that it has won a victory; every great joy carries a note of triumph.[2]

No creature ever comes out perfect from the hands of the Creator; but each receives from Him, according to its nature, the law and the means to tend to its perfection through

---

[1] St. Thomas, *Summa theol.,* IIa IIae, q. 184, a. 2.
[2] H. Bergson, *L'Energie spirituelle,* p. 24.

1

progressive development; each in its turn is equipped and must fight for its fullness of life, for its perfection.

The spectacle of this creative evolution is a magnificent one, starting as it does from primitive chaos, begetting light, heat, and force through the affinities and attractions of the ever moving inorganic world, through the inexhaustible seeds and directive finalities of the living world, through the daring and rational interventions of intelligence and liberty, always rising toward the completion of existence, toward perfection, under the guidance and with the help of the Supreme Being, the Infinite Perfection.

Man leads this progressive march. Properly speaking, he alone, being intelligent and free, acts for his perfection and directs himself toward his end; he alone is capable of enjoying the very beatitude of reaching his destiny; he alone sees and seeks his perfection, his end and beatitude in God, the unlimited Good. Composed of body and soul, kneaded of earth and light, as the Paschal liturgy expresses it, *"nobilem limo jugasti spiritum,"* we need to a certain degree material goods; nature makes us regularly find some pleasure in them in order to incite us to seek them and use them. But unless we are forgetful of the noblest part in us, not to speak of our Christian character, we shall not let ourselves be engulfed in material things nor seek our end and happiness in sensible enjoyments. As St. Augustine forcefully says:

> In what does the good of an animal consist? In eating, in sleeping. . . . You need that yourself and God provides it. But do not stop there. As coheir of Christ would you be able to find your joy in what you have in common with the animal? Raise your aspirations to the Supreme Good![3]

Neither could we find our perfection and happiness in the higher goods of this world such as science, affection, honor,

----

[3] St. Augustine, *De doctr. Christ.,* I, 22.

no matter how valuable and agreeable. Our minds and hearts thirst after unlimited light and love. In this world, our pursuit of truth quickly stumbles before the mysterious, and affections as well as honors often betray us; at any rate, we have to give them up when we die. A soul truly human exclaims with St. Augustine: "You made us for Yourself, O God, and our heart is restless until it rests in You." And again: "You made us so great, O God, that nothing less than You will ever give us peace and happiness."[4] We reach, therefore, our end and perfection when we reach God through knowledge and love, the sole means for spiritual substances to meet and become united.

However, if we were only destined to know and to love God as Creator by the simple exercise of our natural powers, our union with Him would not be the possession of His infinite goodness, nor the sharing of His life and happiness. We should reach Him only from afar, from the outside so to speak, through abstract ideas on the beauty of the created world, and through a love inspired by His natural benefits.

Actually God has deigned to raise our soul and faculties to the supernatural state by the infusion of sanctifying grace and of the virtues, especially faith and charity. This elevation has rendered our heart and soul capable of knowing and loving God as He is, as He knows and loves Himself (One God in Three Persons). We really enter into a participation of His life and happiness; and each new step in faith and charity places us in more perfect possession of His light and goodness, while we wait for the intuitive vision and beatific joy of heaven.

These psychological and theological deductions form the solid and fruitful basis of any treatise on perfection. Nevertheless, to realize fully their truthful and life-giving power we must meditate on them in the light of the dogma of our

---

[4] St. Augustine, *De natura boni*, VIII.

incorporation with Christ. This dogma will be fully developed
in the third volume. Here we mention only the four central
truths of this mystery:

Our eternal election by the Father in His Son, the Word
Incarnate, to a share in His purity, His consecration, His
Sonship.

The Incarnation in time of the Word in Jesus Christ, the
Man who is, in His personal being, the well-beloved Son,
the Holy Priest of the Father, and whose soul is filled to the
brim with graces of light and love.

Our incorporation with Christ through baptism, whose
character, an image of beauty and a title to divine rights,
consecrates us to the Father, while the grace of this sacrament makes us share in the life of the soul of Christ, as the
members of the human body live by the impetus which comes
from the head, as branches live from the sap which flows
from the stock of the vine.

The ever increasing realization of our destiny, of our perfection as Christians and adopted sons of the Father in
proportion to the growth in us of Christ's life of love for
His Father, a life of prayer, of self-abandonment, of zeal,
which constitutes the glory and delight of the Blessed Trinity
in the sanctuary of our soul.

II. *Degrees of Perfection*

The division of the work of our perfection into three
degrees or ways has been a classical one for many centuries.

We find it already in St. Augustine when he says: "Charity;
upon its birth in the soul, is nourished; nourished, it grows
strong; strengthened, it becomes perfect."[5]

The accepted terms of purgative, illuminative, and unitive
ways date at least from St. Bonaventure. He says in his

---

[5] St. Augustine, *In Joan.,* Tr. V.

Itinerarium: "Ascent (to perfection) is made in three stages: the purgative, which consists in the exclusion of sin; the illuminative, which consists in the imitation of Christ, and the unitive, wherein the soul receives the Divine Spouse."[6]

Nowadays, certain authors prefer to substitute for these accepted terms expressions that describe the three *ages* of the soul, infancy, adolescence or youth, and maturity.

It is true that St. Paul himself speaks of "children," still weak in faith; of the "strong," who are growing spiritually, and of the "perfect men," who are attaining the plenitude of Christ. But the Apostle does not pretend to propose or to impose any strict classification of the different conditions of the Christian soul with regard to perfection. These terms are borrowed from several epistles and seem rather to be qualifications applied in passing to certain groups of Christians.[7]

St. Thomas also, in the IIa IIae, q. 24, a. 9, develops the analogy which can be drawn between the progress of the spiritual life and the growth of our natural life. He does not, however, seek in this analogy the principle of distinction between the phases of progress of our spiritual life. He looks for this principle in the degree of the intensity of our fight against the obstacles which oppose in this world our union of charity with God. In a very lofty and very practical article, which we are tempted to quote in full, St. Thomas presents this principle clearly. First, he asks himself "whether anyone can be perfect in this life." The answer is in the affirmative provided we understand well in what perfection consists here below. For there are three kinds of perfection, the perfection of God, that of the saints in heaven, and the one which it is

---

[6] Quoted by Pourrat, *Spiritualité chrétienne* (Paris, 1924), II, 267.

[7] Rom. 14:1; 15:3; Eph. 4:14; 22 f.; Hebr. 5:12 ff.; Eph. 3:16; 4:14 f.; Col. 1:28; Phil. 3:15. Duperray, *Le Christ dans la vie chrétienne, d'apres saint Paul,* 3 ed., 188–190.

possible for men to attain on earth. The perfection which consists in loving God fully and continually, "and answers to a totality not only on the part of the lover, but also on the part of the object loved," is exclusively proper to God, the Infinite Good and Infinite Love. The perfection of the saints in heaven consists of loving God with all their power, yet not according to the depth of His infinite amiability but "according to an absolute totality on the part of the lover, so that the affective faculty always actually tends to God as much as it possibly can."

Finally, there is the perfection here below which cannot comprehend the infinite goodness of the object loved nor is able to exist in a continuous act of love, however limited. It consists in a more or less generous fidelity in removing obstacles to the progress of our love toward God:

> The third perfection answers to a totality neither on the part of the object loved, nor on the part of the lover as regards his always actually tending to God, but on the part of the lover as regards the removal of obstacles to the movement of love toward God. . . . Such perfection can be had in this life.[8]

According to St. Thomas, therefore, the principle which allows us to distinguish here below the different degrees of perfection is not to be sought in more or less sustained continuity of our acts of love, since such a continuity is impossible, but in more or less generous fidelity in removing obstacles which are opposed to the progress of our love for God.

Again, in the same article which we have just analyzed, St. Thomas distinguishes the first two classical degrees of perfection. What constitutes an obstacle to the love of God in our heart, he says, is, first, mortal sin, which is essentially contrary to charity; then, there are the selfish affections which

---

[8] St. Thomas, *Summa theol.*, IIa IIae, q. 184, a. 2.

prevent in varying degrees our union with God by rendering us too much attached to ourselves. The work of the "beginners" is to exclude mortal sin from their souls, while the fight against these selfish affections is the task of "those who are progressing." In a previous question St. Thomas had already linked to the first two degrees, the *Incipientes* and the *Proficientes,* the third one which he called the *Perfecti,* that is, persons whose efforts to detach themselves from mortal sin and from their selfish affections end in a more intimate and loving union with God: ". . . to be united with God and to enjoy Him."[9] The very title of the article enumerates the three degrees: "Whether Charity is Rightly Distinguished into Three Degrees, Beginning, Progress, and Perfection?"

This doctrine of St. Thomas follows the Gospel and the Pauline tradition that impose on us the law of death to sin and to ourselves if we want to live unto God in Christ Jesus. It is the constant reminder of our Lord that we must lose our life and mortify our selfish desires, if we wish to save our soul for the Kingdom of God, the kingdom of charity. "If any man will come after me, let him deny himself, and take up his cross daily, and follow me."[10] And St. Paul: "And do you also reckon, that you are dead to sin, but alive unto God, in Christ Jesus Our Lord."[11] "With Christ I am nailed to the cross. And I live, now not I, but Christ liveth in me."[12] This teaching of St. Thomas is consonant with the very dogma of our incorporation with Christ in His death triumphant over sin and in His life full of love for the Father. And in the light of this dogma we discover the distinctive characteristics of the three classical degrees of perfection.

---

[9] *Ibid.,* IIa IIae, q. 24, a. 9.

[10] Lk. 9:23. Also Mt. 10:39; 16:25; Mk. 3:4; 8:35; Jn. 12:25.

[11] Rom. 6:11.

[12] Gal. 2:19 f. Also Col. 1:9–13; 2:11–15. Cf. Pourrat, *Spiritualité chrétienne* (Paris, 1921), I, 1–25; 25–56.

The first degree is frequently called *conversion of heart:* entire cleansing from mortal sins of the past and preservation from them in the future. It is an attitude of absolute opposition to mortal sin, full of sorrow, if it be necessary, for what is past, and a resolution to avoid sin at any cost in the future. The soul finally understands mortal sin as "aversion from God, our last end," as the "evil of God," since it goes against His goodness by destroying the life of Jesus and His gifts in us. If it has fallen, the soul rids itself of this evil by penance and more particularly by the blood of Jesus, its Saviour. It preserves itself from sin in the future by watching and praying under the guidance and through the grace of Jesus, so as not to fall into the snares of voluntary temptation.

The second degree is variously called *illumination, progress, detachment of heart:* cleansing from venial sins, liberation from inordinate passions, and adornment with virtues. It is a progressive diminution of deliberate venial sin in our life by the fight against the passions and by the acquisition of virtues. Enlightened by faith, the soul finally comes to understand the true malice of deliberate venial sin as opposition to the love of Jesus and to the glory of the Blessed Trinity, who resides in the soul. As a consequence, the soul strives to die more and more to self, since the principle of venial sin is our dominant self-love. At the same time, the soul endeavors to make Jesus live within it through His virtues and His very life.

The third degree is the *perfect union:* An intimate and almost constant union of the soul with God through affective and effective love. It is an intimate and almost continuous association with God by sentiment and especially by act. By overcoming still more her self-love the soul lives in an almost habitual state of filial union with God by a more and more perfect incorporation to Christ.[13]

---

[13] LeGaudier, S.J., *De perfectione vitae spiritualis* (Turin, 1903), I, Chap.

In real life, however, the distinction between the three ways is not as clear cut as we make it in our description. As St. Thomas remarks: The beginners may progress; this is evident since the mere fact of avoiding sin is progress. Yet the chief care that besets them is to resist the onslaught of sin. After-ward, when they feel it less, they think of progress. The perfect, for their part, continue to make progress, and very rapidly; still, this is not their chief care. Their attention is directed less toward advancement in virtue than toward union with God.[14] Actually, then, the three degrees of perfection are one and the same vital movement, the same march of the soul. The ways complete and perfect one another toward greater purification from sin and a more loving union with God. This is why in priestly and religious retreats even the loftiest meditations should always be preceded by a return in some form or other to the fundamental truths of conversion, and should end in practical resolutions for a more profound self-renunciation.

Finally, in the direction of souls let us keep in mind not only this law of continuity which in a certain manner unites and merges the three degrees of the spiritual life, but also let us remember the differences in education, social standing, health of each soul, and particularly the special designs of God and the diversity of the measure of His graces to each individual.

In a small and modest study like the present one we shall avoid the use of modern terminology[15] in describing the first

---

I, 11. DeGuibert, S.J., *Theologia spiritualis ascetica et mystica* (Rome, 1937), pp. 280–322. References to this are to the original Latin edition.

14 St. Thomas, *Summa theol.,* IIa IIae, q. 24, a. 9, ad 2 et 3.

15 The application to the first degree, even, of the spiritual life of expres-sions such as "passive purification of the senses" and "a beginning of infused contemplation," which other authors think should be strictly confined to treatment of the third degree or, at any rate, to the higher reaches of the second.

two ways of the spiritual life. We do not mean thereby to prejudge the value of more recent expressions or to condemn them, but we deem it better to adhere to the older terms *purgative* and *illuminative* way, of fight against sin and self-love by the mortification of the senses and self-renunciation, of the gifts of the Holy Ghost and of the life of Jesus in us. These older terms, perhaps because of their evangelical tone, seem to us clearer, surer, and better adapted to attract souls and to help them toward perfection.

Chapter I 🦋 The Twofold Movement
in True Conversion of Heart

AT THIS first stage of the spiritual life, the soul, in assuming an attitude of opposition to mortal sin, attaches itself to God in a definite manner by love: "Who then shall separate us from the love of Christ? . . . neither death nor life . . . nor things present, nor things to come . . . nor any other creature shall be able to separate us from the love of God, which is in Christ Jesus Our Lord."[1] The first way does not consist merely in the state of grace, or the absence or freedom from mortal sin; it implies a positive movement, a conscious determined attitude of opposition to mortal sin.

The life of grace begins for us at baptism, but baptism is not the beginning of our spiritual life. Is it, indeed, proper to speak of spiritual life at all for a large number of those who have been put through the ceremony of baptism? Hardly had they attained the use of reason when they lost sanctifying grace through mortal sin, and what, indeed, remains in them that is supernatural? A hope — a possibility — or, perhaps better, that last germ which is the virtue of faith, a faith hardly perceptible at times.

At times this germ of faith, by which the sinful soul is kept within the body of the Church, awakens through the assistance of the Communion of Saints and the power of the sacrament of penance, and the soul attains once again the state of grace. But even in the case of those adults who return momentarily to grace, can one speak rightly of spiritual life? Tossed between God and sin, living for a time and then falling back into spiritual death, they waver miserably on the

---

[1] Rom. 8:35–39.

confines of the Kingdom of God. They bring to the tribunal of penance an attrition which justifies the priest in giving them absolution but leaves him with the certitude that they are not truly converted, but will indubitably fall back again into the same sins. No, in the case of such unfortunate souls, one cannot yet speak of spiritual life.[2] DeGuibert classifies among persons not truly converted, although on the way to conversion, children who are just becoming aware of their faults and of their passions; Christians who practice their faith in hardly more than an external manner, without a true appreciation of the place of God in their lives; sinners who desire to do better but are yet too weak or too exposed to be able to free themselves from the bonds of sin.[3] May we not also consider as not yet possessing real spiritual life an adult who, despite the fact that he has attained the use of reason, lives in surroundings so undisturbed, so protected, that his virtue remains intact without effort, without a struggle, almost without his being aware of it?

Real spiritual life begins with conversion. Conversion signifies a decisive choice between sin and God, a step meant to be irrevocable, by which the Christian soul turns away from mortal sin and in a definitive manner attaches itself to God, its supreme good, the one and only object of its love. It is, finally, a beginning of the realization of the first and greatest of the commandments: "Thou shalt love the Lord thy God with thy whole heart, and with thy whole soul, and with thy whole mind, and with thy whole strength."[4] Conversion does not necessarily imply a fall, but a struggle. Only too often, however, a fall into mortal sin does precede true conversion. Most people, indeed, go through two conversions: one imperfect, the other definitive. The first coincides with the

---

[2] Valentin Breton, *Les ages de l'ame,* 14 f.

[3] DeGuibert, *op. cit.,* 291.

[4] Mk. 12:30; Mt. 22:37.

awakening of conscience, turned toward God by baptism but troubled and dragged down by weakness and the passions of early youth. The second, the true conversion, takes place in some cases about the age of twelve, in other cases only at the end of high school or college.

Now, it is true — and for this we should be profoundly grateful to our blessed Lord, and to His Vicar, the fatherly and well-loved St. Pius X — that the early and frequent Communion of little children serves admirably to strengthen the first conversion of these young souls before they have incurred any serious fall. Still, if we are to describe the movement of true conversion in a thorough fashion, and as it is found in most souls, we must consider the attitude of these souls with regard to past sin that conversion causes them to detest and expiate, and with regard to possible sin which they must always fear and avoid in the future.

With Regard to the Past:

A Right Understanding and Detestation of Mortal Sin; The Desire and Effort to Expiate It

"For I know my iniquity and my sin is always before me."[5]

To the soul that has meditated profoundly before God, the mystery of iniquity, the remembrance of its sins, remains ever present, not as the troublesome specter of remorse or the distressing chimera of a scruple, but as a light that gives peace and a grace that purifies. This is the light and grace of true conversion, and how precious, indeed, it is.

The perusal of a pious essay on the malice of mortal sin might make a salutary impression upon us. Struck by a devout meditation or by a powerful mission sermon, we

---

[5] Ps. 51:5.

might approach the sacrament of penance with lively sentiments of contrition; but this impression, these sentiments,
remain superficial and are not lasting. We have not sounded
the abyss of misery hidden in mortal sin: deicide and hell. We
have not yet attained that blessed light which will lead us
finally along the way of true conversion. In mortal sin we
have seen less the offense given to God than the frightful or
troublesome consequences for ourselves. In seeking forgive-
ness from our confessor we were more like Saul than David:

> And Saul said to Samuel: I have sinned because I have trans-
> gressed the commandment of the Lord and of thy words fearing
> the people and obeying their voice. But now bear, I beseech thee
> my sin and return with me that I may adore the Lord. . . . I
> have sinned: yet honor me now before the ancients of my
> people and before Israel and return with me that I may adore
> the Lord thy God.[6]

We appreciate confession and absolution because they save
us from the eternal anger of the Lord. They permit us to
forget our falls, always more or less dishonorable, and to
feel ourselves re-established in our own esteem, worthy to
receive Holy Communion, and once more officially the friends
of God. How far we are from the simple and great word of
the soul truly repentant and truly converted: "I have sinned
against thee my God, to thee only I have sinned and have
done evil before thee."[7] "And David said to Nathan: I have
sinned against the Lord, and Nathan said to David: The Lord
also has taken away thy sins."[8]

The Christian who is truly repentant and converted sees
above all in mortal sin an offense against God. He seeks less
to reinstate himself than to vindicate the sacred rights of the

---

[6] 1 Kings 15:24 f., 30.
[7] Ps. 50:6.
[8] 2 Kings 12:13.

divine Master which have been violated by his malice and pride. He constitutes himself the advocate, the defender of the justice of God. He arms himself with a holy hatred, inspired by love, to crucify his flesh and break his will: "The promoter of God's justice, armed with loving zeal against himself, he avenges his offenses against God in his flesh, in his will, by the practice of mortification."[9]

No longer is the accusation of sins of our past life against this or that virtue just the customary way of bringing our confession to a close; this turning back upon the past is the expression of an increasingly ardent desire for a more thorough cleansing from sin. "Wash me yet more from my iniquity."[10] This turning back upon the past is the result of the profound conviction that it is sweet and gracious for Jesus to be ever more fully our Saviour as He washes us once more in His Blood at each new absolution. Now in our meditation we dwell with delight upon the name of Jesus, our Saviour, upon His title of Lamb of God: "Behold the Lamb of God, behold him who taketh away the sin of the world"[11] by bearing Himself the weight of it to Gethsemani and Calvary. The crown of such a meditation is a communion of expiatory love.

With Regard to the Future:

Realizing Its Own Weakness and Foreseeing the Strength of Temptations, the Soul Is Determined to Do Everything and to Suffer Everything to Avoid Mortal Sin

There are cases of extraordinary conversion which seem to confirm the soul in grace; these are extremely rare and just

---

[9] LeGaudier, op. cit., p. 175.

[10] Ps. 50:4.

[11] Jn. 1:29.

about miraculous. It happens frequently enough, by a special divine grace of God, that a soul which is just turning back to God, even though it was violently tempted and very guilty before, enjoys great peace and profound consolation. When the prodigal returns from afar, the Father is happy to celebrate his arrival.

As a general rule, however, one who has just turned away from sin must expect temptations. He is subject to the common weakness of human nature. There is no one whose virtue is not put to the test, but he who has just turned from sin is the object of more hateful attacks of the enemy, attacks that are aided by images and attachments that rise out of the past, sometimes even in the midst of fervent prayers. There are, moreover, new dangers which a convert might find lurking, as it were, in his more cloistered life, in his studies, in the special duties he must perform. Progress, then, along the purgative way, or solid establishment in conversion, supposes the awareness of our incurable misery, the prevision of temptation, and, finally, the determination to watch and pray not to enter therein since, as we shall explain at length in Chapter VII, the basic, the only danger of relapse is willfully playing with temptation.[12]

---

[12] DeGuibert, *op. cit.*, pp. 296–299.

Chapter II ✤ Assurance and Stability of Conversion

THE NECESSITY, ESPECIALLY FOR THE SEMINARIAN AND THE NOVICE, OF ESTABLISHING HIMSELF FIRMLY IN TRUE CONVERSION

WHY does it sometimes happen that what seems at first a remarkable conversion results at last in an increase of the number of purely nominal Catholics? Because this apparent conversion was really not a conversion at all. Sensible feelings, a love of art, the vagaries of an inquisitive spirit, may indeed sometimes serve to start a person along the road to conversion, but they can never of themselves support a sincere entrance upon a sustained march along the purgative way. They do not give that light which begets a profound conviction with regard to God and sin. They do not inspire the generous efforts necessary to flee the occasions of sin and to crucify our unruly desires.

Here is a consecrated soul who for years now should be standing firmly upon the summits of the second way in luminous faith and total renunciation. Why does it still waver between periods of fervor and laxity, perhaps even between the state of grace and sin? Other explanations may, indeed, be offered besides that of a lack of true conversion from the start, because even after undergoing a sincere turning of the soul toward God during the years of formation, a soul may always fall into the snare of temptation or become prey to lukewarmness. However, more frequently than not, this lack of stability derives from the weakness of the soul's first establishment in the spiritual life. This soul did not enter upon the purgative way with true sincerity, or it did not advance a safe distance along this way.

Perhaps the candidate for the religious life was too young, too lighthearted to profit by the austere graces of the novitiate. The canonical age for entrance into the novitiate does not necessarily coincide with maturity of mind and character. Perhaps he was not fortunate enough to find an experienced guide, wise and firm spiritual direction. Such a deficiency is not an impossibility in independent monasteries with their own individual novitiates. Perhaps the young man, counting presumptuously on his past innocence and yielding to the attraction of passing fervor, rushed his spiritual advance; brushing aside the hidden, troublesome labor of laying the foundations, he made immediately for the heights of a perfection that was little more than a combination of imagination and vanity. Or again, a novice of delicate health may have been babied by his superiors; or still another, subject to interior trials of temptation or scrupulosity, which he was not able to understand, was too distracted or discouraged to undertake the essential work of the purgative way.

The immediate cause is, after all, of small importance. The disastrous effect is always the same. The spiritual structure lacks foundations; it remains weak, shaky, until the basic work is resumed. Patching, even careful patching of the breaks, will never be enough to guarantee the solidity of an edifice without foundation. It is absolutely necessary to lay the foundation again.[1]

Instead of keeping to generalities, let us consider the necessity of real conversion for those aspiring to perfection in the priesthood or in the religious life. This is a question of great practical importance at all times but especially today when, alongside vocations that one might call official — vocations recognized and cultivated over a long period of time in pre-

---

[1] LeGaudier, *op. cit.*, I, 179 f.

paratory seminaries and apostolic schools — there spring up so many others spontaneously, as it were, in colleges and universities, in literary circles and even among men and women engaged in professions and trades. Such vocations are certainly very generous and desirable, but are there not some which are embraced in part out of an airy enthusiasm? Do not some young people, without examination, without direction, seek to scale the heights, though they do not possess the assurances which guarantee the safety of their ascent?

In his encyclical *On the Catholic Priesthood* which so moved the hearts of all priests and indeed of all truly Catholic souls, Pius XI, of happy memory, with special stress, made this the question of the day when he begged bishops and superiors of religious institutes "never to fail in the severity necessary" in the choice and formation of subjects "through fear that the number of priests in the diocese or institute will begin to fall off. . . . One well-trained priest is worth more than a large number with little or no preparation on which the Church can hardly depend at all, if indeed she does not have to weep over them."[2]

The novice, the seminarian, are often considered classical examples of the person who has been "converted": that is, of the soul that has sincerely entered upon the purgative way and is resolutely engaged in advancing therein. Some authors maintain that throughout the whole time of his formation, the novice remains in this way. It is only after his profession, and as a result thereof, that he finds it possible to direct his steps along the illuminative way.[3] It seems to us, on the contrary, that the purpose of the novitiate as presented by

---

[2] Encyclical of His Holiness Pius XI, *On the Catholic Priesthood*, December 20, 1935.

[3] Cf. Lallemant, S.J., 1598–1637, *La Doctrine spirituelle*, Part 2, Sect. 2, Art. 1; edition of 1735, Lyons, pp. 107–116. We cite this ancient edition, rather than the edition enriched with several essays by Father Pottier in 1936, to avoid all question of authenticity. Cf. also Valentin Breton, *op. cit.*, p. 15 f.

the *Code of Canon Law* can be attained only by entrance
upon the illuminative way itself.

> To form the spirit of the novice by the study of the rule and
> constitutions, by devout meditations and assiduous prayer, by
> consideration of all that pertains to the vows and virtues, by
> opportune exercises directed towards the complete eradication
> of all bad habits, the proper control of movements of the soul,
> and the acquisition of virtue.[4]

Are we not much higher here than just an attitude of complete opposition to mortal sin? After all, do not the conferences, the spiritual directions, the great retreats, and especially
the choice graces of this year of benediction conspire in
harmony and divine grace to elevate the soul to a life of
wholehearted faith and renunciation; that is, to the illuminative way?

At any rate, and here there is no room for doubt or discussion, the novice, as also the seminarian, should in the
first place complete the course of the purgative way and arrive
at real conversion.

1. *At What Point Must the Future Priest or Religious Be of Necessity Truly Converted?*

Canon Law sets the length of time strictly required for the
novitiate at one year to the day, and it prescribes that the
perpetual profession must, for validity, be preceded by three
years of temporary vows.[5] Similarly, the law requires that a
candidate for the decisive ordination to the subdiaconate be
twenty-one years old and near the end of the third year of his
course in theology.[6] It is during this canonical period that true

---

[4] Can. 565.
[5] Can. 555, 574.
[6] Can. 975, 976.

conversion will take place. It depends above all on the designs of God for each soul. The degree, the influence, and the action of His grace are something extremely personal and mysterious. It depends also on the measure of one's own generosity. All that can be affirmed is that the process should be completed during the time of formation taken as a whole, that is, during the seminary years up to the subdiaconate or during the novitiate, together, when necessary, with the years at the scholasticate up to the perpetual vows.

We say "when necessary" because from the end of the novitiate, with the profession of the temporary vows, the religious is bound in conscience before God to work at his perfection and to strive to persevere in his vocation.

It is true that canonically, before the Church, the religious remains free to give up his vocation and to return to the world at the end of the temporal vows. It has been the desire of the Church to leave the way open for the exceptional case of the young man who loses his taste for the religious life after the first years of experience. But this kindly tolerance which serves to take care of a delicate situation before it is too late is not meant to render such a situation entirely good and without sin. The Church will not disquiet one who withdraws in these unfortunate circumstances. He is in good standing with her, but she does not excuse this disloyalty before God. In this case she might add to her kindly concessions the clause that is found in certain rescripts of secularization, "Let him look to his conscience." In his time, Father Lallemant also spoke of dispensations with which "the religious is still truly an apostate before God" although in the public eye and — in canonical terminology — *in foro externo* he is in good standing.[7]

When they call a subject to the vows at the end of the novitiate, his superiors consider him fitted for the religious

---

[7] Lallemant, *op. cit.*, pp. 126–127.

life, not for three years only but for life. When the religious pronounced his first vows, he desired to live and die in his institute. Now, indeed, since the instruction of the Sacred Congregation of Religious, *On the Clerical and Religious Formation of Students,* of December, 1931, he must even give open written expression to this desire, "rendering testimony to his vocation to the religious and clerical state and declaring at the same time his firm determination to be enrolled permanently among the clerics in this or that institute."[8] If, then, during the three years of the temporal vows, the intentions of the young religious have changed — that is, outside of exceptional cases beyond his control that constitute a providential trial, such as family misfortunes or need of support, his inability to make the necessary grade in his studies — if in other cases his intentions have changed, it is because he has been unfaithful to grace, because he has not been willing to continue to put forth the effort necessary to persevere in his vocation by persevering in real conversion.[9] We see no need, however, of making any serious modification in what we have

---

[8] *Acta Apostolicae Sedis* (1932), 79.

[9] Some of us may not be inclined to follow the revered author in his contention that temporary vows are temporary only juridically but practically perpetual in spirit and moral obligation. This view would appear to be an application to the New Law of an attitude of mind acquired by the older masters of the spiritual life and canonists when temporary profession was not prescribed. The moral obligation would seem to extend no further than the terms of the vow. Cf. St. Thomas, *Summa theol.,* IIa IIae, q. 189, a. 4. Applicable here would seem to be the pronouncement of Pope Pius XII that there is no disharmony between the internal and external forums, "Allocution to the Rota," October 1, 1942; *Acta Apostolicae Sedis,* 34–338 ff.; Bouscaren, *Canon Law Digest,* III, p. 609 f. It is true that an evil motive would vitiate the act of giving up the religious life after temporary vows but the desire to work out one's salvation in marriage is not an evil motive. The situation is totally different, once one has made perpetual vows.

Differing with Father Grimal on this secondary point, we are heartily in accord with him that a thoroughgoing conversion should take place in the religious or candidate for the priesthood during the years of probation.

said, and we consider as a single period for the establishment of true conversion either the years at the seminary up to the subdiaconate, or the time of the novitiate and scholasticate until the perpetual vows. Still, let it be well understood that a definite decision is reached at the end of the novitiate, that the work of conversion is decided upon in principle. The three years of the temporal vows serve only to strengthen this conversion, either by removing certain weaknesses which flow from youth — lack of reflection, sickness, the dangers of military service — or by bringing about the normal development of this first step through progress along the illuminative way.

2. *The Role of the Spiritual Director in Determining Whether There Exists a Sufficient Guarantee of Real Conversion Such as Is Absolutely Demanded for Religious Vows or for the Subdiaconate.*

We are not concerned here with the call to the vows or to sacred orders in the external forum. It is clear that this call belongs entirely to the major superiors or to the bishop. We consider the role of the spiritual director only in the internal forum, in the realm of conscience and before God. If we were to give them a strictly literal interpretation, independent of traditional practice, two recent documents might lead one to think that the candidate for the vows of Holy Orders is himself in the internal forum the sole judge of his vocation and of the conversion that it necessarily presupposes.

Indeed, according to the instruction of the Sacred Congregation of Religious which we have just cited, the novice should, before his first vows, present to his superiors a written document in which he expressly declares that he considers himself called to the religious and clerical state. "Let them present to the superior a written petition in which they declare

expressly their vocation to the religious and clerical state."
According to a similar instruction of the Sacred Congregation
of the Sacraments to all bishops, "About the testing of candidates before they are promoted to orders," of December 27,
1930, the candidate for sacred orders should, before reception
of each order, declare under oath: "I do spontaneously desire
and of my own full and free will wish to receive the same,
because I know and feel that I am truly called by God."[10]

Without doubt, these two instructions neither deny nor lose
sight of the role of the spiritual director in the internal forum,
but their silence on this point might cause those who have
at heart the long-standing tradition of seminaries and novitiates in the matter of deciding vocations to fear that in the
future too much importance might be attached to these
juridical forms of declaration or oath at the expense of real
interior training, which is the work of spiritual direction.

According to this long-standing tradition each novice, each
seminarian entrusts his soul to a spiritual director whose task
it is to watch over his progress in perfection, and, when the
time comes, to help in the answer which the young man
must make in conscience to the external call of the superiors
or of the bishop. The director does not himself decide the
vocation; nothing is so personal and spontaneous as the
answer of the soul to the call of God. But the director must
guide the young man, must help him to consider, and, if
need be, must reassure him in the solution and answer to
this all important question: Am I morally capable, am I
sufficiently established along the road of true conversion to
take upon myself the obligation of the three vows or of eccle-
siastical celibacy?

It would appear that our Holy Father, Pope Pius XI,
meant to clarify the silence of the two instructions when he

---

[10] *Acta Apostolicae Sedis* (1931), 120–127.

emphasized in his encyclical *On the Catholic Priesthood* the function and the responsibility of the spiritual director, in the internal forum, in the decision of vocations.

This achievement in the erection and management of Seminaries for the education of future priests deserves all praise. But it would be of little avail, were there any lack of care in the selecting and approving of candidates. In this selection and approval, all who are in charge of the clergy should have some part: superiors, spiritual directors, and confessors, each in the manner and within the limits proper to his office. They must indeed foster and strengthen vocations with sedulous care; but with no less zeal they must discourage unsuitable candidates, and in good time send them away from a path not meant for them. . . . Let superiors of seminaries, together with the spiritual directors and confessors, reflect how weighty a responsibility they assume before God, before the Church, and before the youths themselves, if they do not take all means at their disposal to avoid a false step. We declare, too, that confessors and spiritual directors could also be responsible for such a grave error; not indeed because they can take any outward action, since that is severely forbidden them by their most delicate office itself, and often too by the inviolable sacramental seal; but because they can have a great influence on the souls of the individual students, and with paternal firmness they should guide each according to his spiritual needs. Should the superiors, for whatever reason, not take steps or show themselves weak, then especially should confessors and spiritual directors admonish the unsuited and unworthy, without any regard to human consideration, of their obligation to retire while yet there is time; in this they should keep to the most secure opinion, which in this case is the one most in favor of the penitent, for it saves him from a step which could be for him eternally fatal. If sometimes they should not see so clearly that an obligation is to be imposed, let them at least, use all the authority which springs from their office and the paternal affection they have for their spiritual sons, and so induce those who do not have the necessary fitness to retire of their own free will.[11]

His Holiness has reference here to "Italian" or "Tridentine" seminaries, that is, seminaries as founded in Italy according to the decree of the Council of Trent. In this system the professors live outside and come merely for their classes; likewise the confessors (several in number) come from the outside on certain days. In the house live the treasurer in charge of temporal affairs, the superior who is responsible for the general conduct of the seminary, and the spiritual director upon whom, as the encyclical tells us, falls "so important a part in the nurture of the priestly spirit,"[12] through the conferences he gives to the students, through individual direction, or through confession, if the young men come to him.

But neither the Sovereign Pontiff nor the *Codex* by merely mentioning the Italian or Tridentine form of seminaries ever intended to condemn the system known as the Sulpician system. Here the professors reside in the seminary, just as the treasurer and the superior; and they undertake (except the superior, forbidden by can. 981) the role of confessors of the students who desire to entrust to them the direction of their conscience and their interior preparation for the priesthood.[13] Such a system has been adopted by many diocesan and religious seminaries throughout the world.

Recently, in order to conform to the Code (can. 588) and to special directions from Rome, an official master or spiritual director has been introduced in these seminaries. But the system has not been substantially modified by this change, since the seminarians continue to choose from the resident

---

[11] *Acta Apostolicae Sedis*, 28 (1936), 39, and 41.

[12] *Ibid.*, 37.

[13] Blouet, S.S., *La communaute educatrice du clerge de France*, Paris, 1915.

faculty, when its members are religious,[14] the confessor to whom they entrust the guidance of their souls.

Our preferences are for this system which has proved its worth during the past centuries and which embodies an ideal which the Council of Trent dared not impose. It was left for St. Vincent de Paul, St. John Eudes, and Father Olier, men providentially raised for the reform of the clergy, to bring it to realization.

What occurs in the novitiate confirms our preferences. The New Code, at the same time that it imposes upon the master the spiritual direction of the novices (can. 565), forbids him to hear their confessions, unless it be in exceptional cases for urgent and grave reasons: "Unless the students for a grave and urgent reason, in exceptional cases, fully seek it" (can. 891). Consequently, the novices who really desire direction must equivalently go to confession to two persons: to the official confessor to receive absolution in the holy tribunal of penance, and to the master himself in the intimacy of their personal talks with him, since he has the right to expect and encourage these manifestations of conscience.[15] We may add that the novices, in their desire to be better known and better guided in deciding their vocation and their work toward perfection, will find a grave and urgent reason to come to the master for confession during the time of the four great retreats. For in practice it is very difficult to separate entirely true spiritual direction from confession.[16]

[14] Sacred Congregation of Seminaries and Universities, January 24, 1928; in Bouscaren, *Canon Law Digest,* I, 651.

[15] Cf. *Commentarium pro Religiosis,* V (1924), 159–161, and VI (1925), 25 f.

[16] The master is forbidden to hear habitually the confessions of the novices because of the anxiety to keep separate two jurisdictions, which ought to be distinct, the jurisdiction of conscience and the jurisdiction of the external call to profession. This danger of mixing and confusing the two jurisdictions was not overlooked by the ancient legislation and particularly by the

In any system whatever, the role of the spiritual director — and of the confessor, if direction is separate from confession — seems to us of capital importance in judging the reality of the conversion which is absolutely required for the vows or the subdiaconate.

3. How or Under What Conditions Is the Spiritual Director Able to Recognize Whether the Aspirant to the Vows or the Subdiaconate Is Truly Converted?

We can suppose three cases that are typical:

The first one, of a young man who has preserved his baptismal innocence;

The second, of a young man who while a boy has committed serious faults, but since the days of his preparatory studies is solidly established in virtue;

Constitution of Clement VIII, *Cum regularem,* of March 19, 1603, which still remains the basis for the internal operation of novitiates (can. 558–565). This legislation supposed nevertheless that in order really to form the novices the master should be their ordinary confessor. It saw in this great and general good of the true formation of future religious a motive sufficient to risk, in accidental cases, the danger of mixing the two jurisdictions. Cannot the priests who were masters of novices before the New Code bear witness to the fact that a providential guidance or a grace of state made such cases quite rare and easy to solve? As we pointed out, however, in the new legislation the master is equivalently and by necessity a confessor. The danger still remains, as the possibility of abuse remains in any divine ministry entrusted to human weakness. To suppress it we would have to do away with the interior formation of the novices by the master.

Of late great stress has been laid on insuring at any cost freedom for the novices and seminarians to seek and demand a confessor of their own choice. Well and good. Yet we must remember that when there is question of religious and sacerdotal vocations this principle of freedom of choice of confessors is subject to certain restrictions due to the supreme interests of the Church as well as those of the aspirant himself. Pius XI remembered these restrictions when he insisted so forcefully on the responsibility of the confessors of future priests. The confessor or director assumes this responsibility before God only when the young man has been faithful and loyal to open his conscience to the director or confessor and permit him to study for a sufficient time the progress of his spiritual life.

Finally, the case of a young man who continues to fall more or less frequently into serious faults, or who at least exposes himself in such a manner as to experience afterward serious uneasiness of conscience.

These typical cases refer principally to chastity, as this virtue is admittedly a very difficult problem in the formation and call of a great many young men. It should not be, however, the only question. Perhaps — the remark was made over thirty years ago by Bishop LeCamus in a letter on the moral training of seminarians — perhaps certain directors are overly concerned with the question of chastity. Serious and constant attention should be given to other virtues, even in the case of young men who are somewhat weak in this particular regard. What a misfortune if instead of forming the entire priest, the years of the seminary were spent to make a man chaste! Besides, is it possible to lead a young man to perfect chastity without raising him to a high level of faith, of confidence, of obedience? Therefore, even though we refer principally to chastity, we shall not overlook the other virtues. This will be clearly seen in the solution of the third case, the only one that is really troublesome.

First Case: With Regard to a Young Man Who Has Preserved His Baptismal Innocence

After the example of the rich young man who came to Jesus with the vital question: "Good master, what good shall I do that I may have life everlasting?" our aspirant could answer on hearing the different commandments: "All these have I kept from my youth."[17] The Gospel, speaking of that young man so noble and so unspoiled, adds: "And Jesus, look-

_____
[17] Mt. 19:16–20.

ing on him loved him."[18] Yes, Jesus loved him; yet, some
commentators, Newman among them in one of his *Parochial
and Plain Sermons,* are severe and almost dislike the young
man. They judge him thoughtless and basically selfish even
at the moment when he approaches Jesus. Unfortunately he
lacked generosity and missed a magnificent opportunity to
follow our Lord. He deserves our pity.

But is it not true that some spiritual writers and certain
directors view young people who come unspoiled to the novitiate or to the seminary with the same severity and suspicions
that such commentators have toward the young man in the
Gospel? LeGaudier[19] imagines in these young people a
natural inclination or disposition rather than true and solid
virtue. They have remained good because they have not had
an occasion to become spoiled. But in the face of dangerous
temptations they would not have the strength to resist. Unhappily, we have heard distinguished directors of seminaries
echo these sentiments. They have a general distrust of those
whom they call "twenty-year-old children" and they are
inclined to consider them ignorant rather than strong.

We have already noted that early and frequent Communion
seems in our days to throw new light on this question. The
Host sanctifies and strengthens the baptismal innocence of
these young men. Their preservation, that is their life in
Jesus, becomes more and more at each Communion a matter
of conscience and personal effort. So much so, that when the
critical period of adolescence arrives they are warned and
armed to defend and preserve their virtue. Any young man
who has remained pure is a strong and virtuous person.

If it should happen that in such souls there still exists
some ignorance or dangerous immaturity, if their goodness of
character tends to degenerate into weakness, if vanity hides
from them the persistence of their lower nature and could

[18] Mk. 10:21.   [19] *Op cit.,* p. 179 f.

lead them on to presumption, their director at the novitiate or seminary and, more especially, the love and grace of our Lord, are there to enlighten, strengthen, and help these privileged souls.

It will be the duty of the director to watch especially over the danger in which these souls find themselves of being impressed prematurely by the attraction of the higher ways. He will wisely keep them, for a time at least, in the humble exercises of the purgative way. Divine Providence may perhaps test them by trials they did not suspect. And we could rightly speak of the "night of the senses" to describe the special action of the Holy Ghost as He guides these chosen souls toward perfect spiritual detachment, self-contempt, and self-distrust.

Second Case: With Regard to a Young Man Who While a Boy Has Fallen Into Serious Faults, but Who Since the Days of His Preparatory Studies Is Solidly Established in Virtue

This young man is truly converted. There remains only to confirm his purpose by keeping him for a while in the purgative way. The exercises themselves of the novitiate or the seminary, his constant and generous effort toward self-renunciation in the illuminative way, will produce a daily increase of grace and strength which will, more than anything else, further his conversion.

Third Case: With Regard to a Young Man Who Continues to Fall More or Less Frequently Into Serious Faults, or, at Least, Who Exposes Himself in Such a Manner as to Experience Afterward Serious Uneasiness of Conscience

As we remarked, this case is really troublesome and, at times, even distressing for the spiritual director. The principle is very clear: only those young men can be admitted to sacred orders or to profession whose purity has either been *preserved* by a conscious effort, or sufficiently *redeemed* by atonement and fight against self, in such a manner as to give moral certitude of their perseverance. Yes, the principle itself is quite clear. But when can we have moral certitude in the case we have presented?

Theologians, according to the nature and the frequency of the faults, indicate periods of time, varying between six months and two years, during which our young man should have preserved himself successfully from any sin of impurity. They add, however, that such indications of material time do not form a sufficient basis for certitude. To arrive at moral certitude that a young man will persevere, we should, they tell us, pay attention especially to his temperament, his effort to correct himself, and his life of piety. This means in reality that the director should endeavor to discover in the young man the essential elements of true conversion. Time is merely a secondary element, a simple condition, although an indispensable one, to judge prudently about this conversion.

Temperament

This first element is rather a negative one. A good temperament in itself and, above all, by itself is not an assurance of perseverance. Nevertheless certain unstable or odd temperaments are an almost infallible sign that God does not call them to undertake the serious burden of religious or priestly obligations.

Thus, a young man should be counseled to leave if he shows an emotional and soft character, prone to special friendships, and who does not fight against this danger and even refuses, through lack of judgment and solid piety, to recognize it, or who fights feebly against it, as a matter of form, because his director forces him to do so.

On the other hand, the director can allow a young man to continue who is conscious of these weaknesses and sees their danger, and who possesses a right judgment and a docile mind together with solid piety. The director can allow him to continue, but he must warn him of the duty of watching constantly and sacrificing himself until death.

A young man of exceptionally nervous and almost hysterical temperament should be advised not to continue. The case is not a rare one among youths of dipsomaniac ancestry. In the face of temptation they will be, as it were, fatally overcome by familiarity with sin and the obsession of defeat. The necessity of daily sacrifice will produce in them sadness, which, to say the least, is a very poor counselor. Yet, many a time, in moments of fervor, such a young man will insist that he has a vocation, that he is ready to make any promises because he has an irresistible impression that God calls him, that he will be happy only in the priesthood or in the religious state.

To allow a young man with a very nervous temperament to make his profession or to receive the subdiaconate we must look for a counterbalancing trait, for security, such as intelligence above the average, a pronounced liking for serious studies, some lofty views and aims, but chiefly a great spirit of faith and confidence in God, deep humility and wholehearted docility to his director and superiors. At times, to offset more effectively those hereditary defects, the young man should add to these superior gifts of mind and to these special graces the irrevocable resolution to build up his physical strength and, for instance, by "taking the pledge," to avoid whatever might prove detrimental to him.

Effort at Self-Correction

We have now entered the field of true conversion. For

indeed, in the present case, what does this word, "self-correction," imply but a sustained and loyal effort to realize at last the evil of sin, to purify oneself from it, to atone for past sins, to avoid or remove every occasion of sin in the future?

We should, after some months of patient and fatherly exhortations, invite to leave the seminary or religious life a young aspirant who continues to fall rather frequently into mortal sin, and who does not take, or takes only indifferently, the means to correct himself, namely, prayer, vigilance, and work. We should give particular attention to the ardor or the absence of reaction after a fall. We have grounds to hope if the young man rises immediately by a good confession and a generous reparation; but there is little hope if he lives at ease for a few days after a fall, waiting until his usual day for confession. And above all we should judge very severely anyone who, through human respect, "to do as the others do," would have the sad courage to approach, some times repeatedly, the holy table in the state of mortal sin.

Likewise the director should not hesitate to counsel a man to leave who falls only rarely into serious sins but who habitually disregards the rule and neglects his exercises of piety as well as his important duty of study. Ordinarily, indeed, such disregard and neglect are accompanied by presumption and audacity in the face of the temptation that arises from certain books, daydreams, or friendships which at first sight appear inoffensive. The young man will not know whether he has sinned gravely on any given occasion. Neither will his director; but the latter knows very well, and should say it, that this imprudent playing with temptation is the fatal way that one day will end in mortal sin. Therefore, such a candidate should leave despite his promises to do better later on, his hopes to be strong when he becomes a priest, despite his avowal of attachment to his vocation, an avowal which is often prompted by human motives.

We quote another passage from the encyclical of Pius XI, *On the Catholic Priesthood,* which confirms our practical conclusions and goes even further than they:

His watchful and experienced eye will perceive, without difficulty, whether one or other have, or have not, a true priestly vocation. This . . . is established not so much by some inner feeling or devout attraction, which may sometimes be absent or hardly perceptible, but rather by a right intention in the aspirant, together with a combination of physical, intellectual, and moral qualities which fit him for such a state of life. He must look to the priesthood solely from the noble motive of consecrating himself to the service of God and the salvation of souls; he must likewise have, or at least strive earnestly to acquire, solid piety, perfect purity of life, and sufficient knowledge. . . . Thus he shows that he is called by God to the priestly state. Whoever, on the other hand, urged on, perhaps, by ill-advised parents, looks to this state as a means to temporal and earthly gains which he imagines and desires in the priesthood, as happened more often in the past; whoever is intractable, unruly, or undisciplined, has a small taste for piety, is not industrious, and shows little zeal for souls; whoever has a special tendency to sensuality, and after a long trial has not proved he can conquer it; whoever has no aptitude for study and who will be unable to follow the prescribed courses with due satisfaction; all such cases show that they are not intended for the priesthood. By letting them go on almost to the threshold of the sanctuary, superiors only make it even more difficult for them to draw back; and, perhaps, even cause them to accept ordination through human respect, without vocation and without the priestly spirit.[20]

---

[20] *Acta Apostolicae Sedis,* 28 (1936), 40.

Life of Piety

By a life of piety we mean something much more than impeccable fidelity to the spiritual exercises of the novitiate or of the seminary. We mean most of all the spirit of faith and the spirit of confidence in Jesus, our Saviour. For this trait is like the light of the purgative way and the soul of true conversion.

A young man could, during the entire period of his training, avoid carefully the occasions of sin, work satisfactorily, and be regular in his life; he could thus spend months and years without falling into serious faults; and yet not give all the guarantees of real conversion and perseverance. If he does not acquire a real spirit of piety, a lively faith, and a loving confidence in our Lord, these habits of prayer, work, regularity, and watchfulness will not last long when he is no longer aided by the safeguards and restrictions of the period and houses of formation. They were practices shaped by the surroundings; it was a superficial virtue, a mere varnish. A true interior life was needed to make it last. We do not say that we would encourage such an aspirant to leave immediately. But we would not rest until we had led him to desire and follow a true life of piety.

On the other hand, an aspirant of rich and ardent nature, may, momentarily, be led to fail in regularity and obedience. They are passing faults, they are recognized immediately and quickly atoned for. He may even, in some fortuitous circumstances, be violently tempted by his vivid imagination or his impressionable temperament and in a passing moment, forgetting the law of vigilance and prayer, enter into temptation, a step which produces in him and in his director some uneasiness of conscience that is not altogether without foundation. But being loyal and discerning, he examines himself thoroughly and opens his soul in all simplicity to his director. Taking into account his ever present attraction for sin, his presumption, he endeavors to acquire a more sincere and strict mistrust of self. Seeing himself always weak, he strives to attach himself with heart and soul to Jesus, his Saviour and Strength. His exercises of piety will not be for him mere duties of rule that he must fulfill in conscience, but they will become more and more life-giving needs and duties of love centered around the Host.

Briefly, this young man has led during the time of his training a life that has been less regular, much less exempt from temptations and faults than was the case with the young man mentioned above. Nevertheless, while we would hesitate and wait for new proofs of the unshaken conversion of the latter, we would unhesitatingly call our ardent aspirant, for he has already given us full guarantee of true conversion and perseverance. He possesses a knowledge of his weakness, a mistrust of self, and a lively and firm trust in Jesus. He leads a true life of piety, a real spiritual life. He will have to fight, but he will conquer; and this very struggle will render him more humble and more strong through the virtue and love of Jesus — Victim in the Holy Eucharist.

Chapter III ❧ The Light of Conversion, Its Nature and Object

THE victory of the love of God over sin, which constitutes real conversion, is not the result of a purely natural effort, nor the culmination of a simple psychological development. This victory is pre-eminently the fruit of grace, a grace which by enlightening the mind strikes powerfully at the will.

We know very well that sin cannot be identified with inattention or error in the mind. It is essentially an act of the will which rises up against the will of God and rejects His love. But we know likewise that this revolt of the will is preceded by, and mixed with, a certain amount of darkness and deviation of the mind. It might be added that these deviations or obscurities of the mind are themselves more or less imputable to an anterior sinful will. If it be true that I will as I think, it is likewise true that I think as I will. Happily we do not have, at this time, to dismantle the complex mechanism of the reciprocal influence of the intellect and will in a human act either in itself or under the allurement of sin and the acts of grace. We remain in the practical field and in this field our analysis attains more frequently the acts of the intellect than of the will. That is why we speak rather of a grace of light; but let it be well understood that this grace does not enlighten the mind except to strike with equal power at the will. We shall study separately the nature and the object of this grace of light.

I. *The Nature of the Light of Conversion*

According to LeGaudier and Lallemant the grace of conversion is reducible in a special way to three gifts of the Holy

Ghost: understanding, wisdom, and counsel. The reason these authors give is that these three gifts are more directly opposed to the threefold deordination which prepares the way for sin: ignorance, perversion of judgment, and inconsideration.[1] In the framework built up by these accepted masters of the spiritual life, the acts of evil and the acts of grace in our own days will easily find their place. Neither the ways of human misery nor the ways of divine mercy change substantially with the passage of time.

First, let us consider ignorance, more or less culpable, of the things of God and of the evil of sin and the gift of understanding. There are different degrees of ignorance. By opposing confession Protestantism removed at one stroke from many of its followers the consciousness of guilt, the true appreciation of sin. How many Catholics there are, Catholics in name only, in whom the seed of faith is buried under worldly interests and earthly views, and whose conscience is almost entirely mute. A large number of practicing Catholics pass easily from the state of grace to the state of sin, because with their glance fixed on earthly horizons and their hearts attached to material goods, they do not see the malice of sin, the one evil in God's sight; for them sin is, at most, an unlawful action or pleasure that one must confess before going to Communion, to avoid sacrilege, and before dying, to avoid hell. Among our Catholic youth, brought up, many of them, in a Christian manner, and aspiring it may be, to perfection, how many there are who consider themselves solidly established in virtue and generous in the service of God, but who lack the real spirit of humility and sacrifice because they have never looked deeply into the mystery of their own weakness and the mystery of expiation in the light of the true nature of sin.

---

[1] LeGaudier, *De perfectione vitae spiritualis*, I, pp. 207–251; Lallemant, *La Doctrine spirituelle*, pp. 218–261, *passim*.

The gift of understanding is in direct opposition to this form of ignorance.

This gift should in effect enable us to form a correct idea and to conceive a proper esteem of our last end and all that is connected therewith. It frees us from a mean estimate of spiritual things. Such an estimate considers them according to earthly views and ends. It belittles, disparages, the most sublime grace that God has bestowed, the greatest sacraments, considering as it does their import, their advantages, only in relation to ourselves and our life here below. The gift of understanding considers God, His graces, ourselves, and our whole life in the radiance of the true light: our last end, heaven, eternity: *Of what profit is this for eternity? Of what value is this in relation to God?* Only that which is eternal lasts long enough for me. "What will it profit me to gain the whole world if I suffer the loss of my soul?" God alone is good; sin alone is evil because it is opposed to God.

Next we examine the more or less culpable perversion of the moral judgment and the gift of wisdom. The perversion of the moral judgment: it is always the same story: ". . . because the light is come into the world, and men loved darkness rather than the light: for their works were evil. For every one that doth evil hateth the light. . . ."[2] This divinely inspired word is confirmed every day by all those perversions of the moral judgment that are brought about by passion. Public opinion tends to justify and exalt certain sins which appeal to pride and sensuality, these being sins which touch the so-called "point of honor." Sins of passion are considered natural, courageous, noble.

So weak are human hearts in this regard that a whole literature may be built up and developed through the description of sin under the seductive lights of a mystic sensualism. We recall the letter of the Holy Office of May 3, 1927, to all

---

[2] Jn. 3:19 f.

bishops of the Catholic world on the "sensual and sensual-mystic type of literature." This letter declares that neither poetic license nor beauty of style nor a claim of good intentions can ever justify such a provocation. Still, so-called Catholics let themselves be won over to this sacrilegious prostitution of talent and religious feeling.[3]

Closer home, a ruling interest that has achieved too strong a grip on our hearts is sufficient to cause us to question the most sacred theory, to disregard the most elementary duties, to justify the most foolhardy imprudence and the most dangerous satisfactions.

The gift of wisdom is directly opposed to this perversion of the moral judgment. The gift of wisdom attacks the very principle of this perversion, an affection or passion which draws us toward evil and causes the mind to justify it. As long as passion or attachment has the upper hand, the soul is unable to judge and condemn its sins. Passion hides from it the evil against God, against oneself and others, included in sin. For the soul to perceive this evil there is need of a light that will penetrate the heart and gradually destroy the love which it has for the object of its sin. There is need of a light that will enable the heart to feel the nearness of God and to enjoy the sweetness of His presence. This light is the gift of wisdom.

> The gift of wisdom is a knowledge of God, and, as it were, a relish for Him. . . . It appreciates God, His grandeur, His beauty, His perfection . . . as infinitely adorable and lovable. Out of this knowledge is engendered a delightful relish for God. . . . There are some souls so upright that they have no taste but for what is good. . . . This is the characteristic effect of wisdom which so fills the soul with a relish for what is good . . . that it can feel only distaste for all other objects.[4]

---

[3] *Acta Apostolicae Sedis* (1927), 186 f.
[4] Lallemant, *op. cit.*, pp. 219, 222 f.

Then perversion of judgment is replaced by uprightness, but an uprightness that is loved, relished by the heart: *recta sapere*. Then the soul tends toward what is good, toward God as to its connatural object, *secundum quamdam connaturalitatem . . . ad res divinas,* according to St. Thomas.[5]

Finally, we compare the more or less culpable lack of consideration of the evil of sin and the gift of counsel. Though well informed of his duties and penetrated by the light which comes from the last end, though free of all passion and with a heart set upon God, man can still easily enough fall into sin if he is thoughtless. How numerous and powerful are the causes which prevent us from giving due consideration to the rights of God and the evil of sin. Because of levity, susceptibility, timidity, or human respect, illness or simple nervous fatigue, "we just do not think."

The gift of counsel is directly opposed to this inconsideration. This gift, in fact, frees us from that haste, that impetuosity which causes us to act under the influence of our natural inclinations or under the influence of our passing impressions, instead of consulting the Holy Spirit.[6]

> The gift of counsel has to do with the guidance of particular acts. It is a light by which the Holy Spirit points out what is to be done in the time, place, and circumstances in which one finds himself. . . . If this gift is wanting to us, we shall not accomplish anything except with many faults and our whole manner of acting will be purely human.[7]

II. *The Object of the Light of Conversion*

The light of conversion shows us that there are only two realities which last forever and which alone matter for us: God and sin. To speak more correctly there is only one

---

[5] St. Thomas, *Summa theol.,* IIa IIae, q. 45, a. 2.

[6] Lallemant, *op. cit.,* p. 260.

[7] Lallemant, *op. cit.,* pp. 250–253.

reality that lasts forever, namely, God. Sin is but a privation, the loss of God. But if we have the misfortune to die in the state of sin we shall experience the consequences of this loss of God forever; in this sense sin, likewise, is for us an eternal reality. This, then, is the sole purpose of our human existence: to serve God and to avoid sin. This is the last word of Ecclesiastes: "Fear God and keep his commandments: for this is all man."[8]

Now, of course, we believe in God and we know that the only evil we need fear is sin, but so long as the light of conversion has not touched our soul, how far we are from measuring and experiencing the full import of life and death contained in these two words: God and sin.

God is the supreme, the unique reality in our life. Even if it were a question merely of obtaining for ourselves or of giving others a solid conviction of the existence of God, we ought to know that the proofs of God's existence are not a philosophy of the mind but a philosophy of objective truth. They rest not upon the laws of thought but upon the law of being. They are not derived from a predisposition on the part of our faculties to create various systems of explanations. On the contrary, they are imposed upon the faculties by the fact of the existence of the universe, a fact which is at one and the same time undeniable and yet clearly insufficient as an explanation of itself. The proofs of the existence of God lead us to the supreme fact, to the supreme reality, which alone can explain the undeniable and otherwise inexplicable existence of the universe.

Cardinal Newman, in his *Grammar of Assent,* wishes to include still other considerations in the proofs for the existence of God, for in man we are led immediately to a God who is not only the Creator of the universe but also the Legislator indispensable for our moral life and the Father

---
[8] Eccles. 12:13.

toward whom rise all the aspirations of our hearts. Naturally, we are not going to discourse here on the arguments for or against Newman's view with regard to the philosophical proofs for the existence of God, but as regards life, the supernatural life, as regards conversion and also the light of union, we follow and indeed we go beyond the thought of Newman.

The light of conversion, placing our minds and hearts in contact with the classical arguments for the existence of God, will make us find there and feel our nothingness, our ignorance, and our complete dependence in the presence of Infinite Majesty, Infinite Wisdom, Infinite Power. We shall feel in the forceful words of Father Faber: "What it is to be a creature. What it is to be a Creator." We shall feel ourselves constantly under the hand of God, our Maker, our Master. One who has this experience "is not far from being a saint"; he has only to be logical to the end.[9]

As Newman has already done in the name of reason and conscience, so my faith and my heart under the action of the light of conversion will seek in God a Lawmaker and a Father: a Legislator who establishes the laws of holiness, a Father who takes us as His sons and gives us life in Jesus His only-begotten Son. It is only at this point that we can be truly converted because it is only here that we come into contact with the goodness of God in a way that is able to call forth all our love.

A supposition, fantastic and impossible though it is, may serve to clarify this thought. If there existed two Gods equally perfect in themselves, one of whom created us and sanctified us, whereas the other gave us absolutely nothing, did not even think of us: this latter God would not count for us. He would have no right over us. He might be considered as nonexistent so far as we should be concerned. St. Thomas declares even

[9] W. Faber, *Creator and Creature,* Book I, Chaps. 2 and 3.

more forcefully: "If God were not our Sovereign Good, we should not find in Him reason to love Him."[10] What makes God count for us, exist for us, what makes Him be good toward us with all His right to our service and love, is surely His infinite perfection. But His infinite perfection considered not in itself, but with regard to us, as it is good for us through the gifts of creation and sanctification. Undoubtedly, the principle of every gift is the infinite perfection in itself, and the object of our cult and love is also this infinite perfection considered in itself. But if it had not bestowed its gifts upon us, we would not be forced to recognize it, to adore it, to love it. We would be unable to do so since we exist only through its gifts.

The light of conversion will lead us, then, to God as recognized, adored, and loved in Himself and in His gifts. To reveal to us the fullness of the existence and goodness of God toward us, this light must raise us to the very mystery of the love of the Father for us in Christ Jesus, the mystery of our eternal election in Christ: the incarnation of the Word in the God-Man, the Son of the Father, full of grace and truth, who comes to make us share in the effusions of His fullness; our incorporation in Baptism to His loving Sonship, His consecration, His life of grace and virtue.

In this light with regard to God, the supreme, the unique reality of our life, we will try to measure the evil of mortal sin, such as it is described in the definitions of St. Augustine and St. Thomas.

The Definition of St. Augustine

Peccatum est dictum, vel factum, vel concupitum contra legem aeternam.[11] Sin is any word, action, or desire against the eternal law. This is the definition used in our catechisms: Sin

---

[10] St. Thomas, *Summa theol.*, IIa IIae, q. 26, a. 13, ad 3.
[11] St. Augustine, *Contra Faustum*, Book 22, Chap. 27.

is any thought, word, deed, or omission against one of the commandments of God or of the Church. The definition applies both to venial and to mortal sin. Restricting it here to mortal sin, we could condense it in this way: A grave violation of the law or of the will of God.

God, our Lord and Master, because of His infinite goodness and rights, imposes upon us laws which He deems necessary for the fulfillment of His plan of justice and holiness. And we, who came from nothing, who receive all from Him, would use His very gifts, our intelligence, our will, our strength, other creatures around us, to go against God and to overthrow His plan. We would oppose our views and our will to His wisdom and authority, which condemn pride, lying, calumny, and impurity as evil. We would oppose His wisdom and authority, which judge and praise chastity, charity, sincerity, and humility as good. We consider good for us and choose to do what God condemns. We consider evil for us and refuse to do what He commands. The plan of God is upset and cast aside each time we choose to live according to our evil inclinations; each time, as if we were their masters, we make ourselves the end of the gifts which God has entrusted to us for His service, of the persons and things that were given to help us.

It is the continuation of the words of revolt that brought the first sin into the world:

> And [the serpent] said to the woman: Why hath God commanded you, that you should not eat of every tree of paradise? And the woman answered him saying: of the fruit of the trees that are in paradise we do eat; but of the fruit of the tree which is in the midst of paradise, God hath commanded us that we should not eat; and that we should not touch it, lest perhaps we die. And the serpent said to the woman: No, you shall not die. . . in what day soever you

shall eat thereof . . . you shall be as gods, knowing good and evil.[12]

The tempter was too wise to speak or to think of making himself equal to God, the Creator and Providence of the universe. Temptation leads to and stops on the grounds of moral independence. It resolves itself to this: You can discern and freely choose what will be good or evil for you; free from the authority of the Lord, you will be the masters and gods of your conduct.

Such was the willful thought that inspired and led to the first mortal sin ever committed in this world; such is the willful thought that leads to every mortal sin committed here; to exclude God, to substitute self for God, to act as if we were gods in the conduct of our moral life.

We can already begin to fathom this fundamental disorder, this rejection of God, this revolt against God, contained in mortal sin: "For I know my iniquity . . . to thee only have I sinned."[13]

The Definition of St. Thomas

This definition will help us penetrate more deeply into the mystery of the iniquity of mortal sin. We borrow the formula of Cardinal Billot, but the ideas are from St. Thomas: *Aversio a Deo fine ultimo per voluntariam conversionem ad bonum commutabile.* It is usually translated: "Aversion from God, our last end, and conversion to a created or changeable good." Yet, to get the full force that is contained in this short but rich formula, we should say: In mortal sin the soul turns away from God its last end, and attaches itself voluntarily to a created being, making this being its end.[14]

---

[12] Gen. 3:1–5.
[13] Ps. 50:6.
[14] L. Billot, S.J., *Disquisitio de natura et ratione peccati personalis,* Rome, 1897, pp. 35–37. This definition does not appear textually in St. Thomas, at

We are here in the core itself of the moral order, in the question concerning the last end, the Supreme Good who demands an absolute and everlasting love. Mortal sin transfers this love from God to a creature, making this creature the concrete object of sin. And on its part, this concrete object becomes the supreme good, the last end, the god for the soul that commits the sin. In reality, therefore, the question of mortal sin resolves itself into a question of love. The supreme love of our heart is refused to God or taken from Him, and is transferred and given to the object of our passion, of our sin. Yes, the fundamental malice of mortal sin is not so much the revolt against the rights of God, our Master, as the contempt and denial of His infinite goodness toward us. As we mentioned already, the rights and the dominion of God over us are, in the last analysis, based on His infinite goodness toward us. To sin, to revolt against the rights of God, is to ignore His goodness, to disregard His love, and to refuse Him ours: "By sin, indeed, by which we are turned from our last end, we practically renounce, so far as in us lies, God's supreme amiability."[15]

In a word, sin is the violation of the first and, so to speak, the only commandment: "Thou shalt love the Lord thy God with thy whole heart, and with thy whole soul, and with thy whole mind, and with thy whole strength."

Some Objections Against These Dogmatic Conclusions on the Evil of Mortal Sin

I. The analysis of mortal sin which we have just presented may be true in certain faults against the first commandments,

least not in the *Summa*. But its two essential elements (aversion from God our last end by our attachment to a created good which becomes our end) appear constantly in the detailed analysis which the holy doctor makes of sin in the Ia IIae from Question 71 to Question 89. See in particular Question 72, Art. 5.

[15] M. de la Taille, S.J., *Mysterium fidei*, 1 ed., p. 26, note 1.

faults of pride, blasphemy, hatred of God. For in committing these sins the soul actually thinks of God, turns itself formally from Him, and, in a way, challenges Him. But in the case of other mortal sins, of pure omissions, of mere moments of weakness, or of rashness under the allurements of passion, the thought of God is so vague and so remote that we cannot legitimately speak of revolt against His goodness, of aversion to His love.

This objection seems to suppose that when we speak of disregarding God's goodness, of aversion to His love, we mean that the sinner turns away *formally* and *directly* from God, the Supreme Good and the Last End of every being. Such a movement of the will would be impossible; the will would attach itself positively to nothing; now, no one can love and desire nonentities. The sins of pride, of blasphemy, of hatred of God, do not challenge the Supreme Good as such, or the Last End as such. They, too, seek some particular good, *bonum commutabile,* such as glory before an unbelieving world, or some sort of feeling of revolt or of anticipated revenge against the constraint of the divine law or against the sanctions of eternal justice. And it is in the pursuit of this particular good that aversion from the Supreme Good and from the Last End are included, even in sins of pride, of blasphemy, of hatred of God.[16]

With greater reason, we do not pretend to discover a direct aversion or a formal rejection of God, our Supreme Good and Last End, in the faults of omission or of passion which are the ordinary forms of mortal sin. But behind the omission, in the center itself of the passion, there is a positive good (a particular amusement, a friendship, an occupation) which we perceive more or less clearly as contrary to the commandments of God, as an occasion for a serious fall, as exposing us to

---

[16] Cf. St. Thomas, *Summa theol.,* Ia IIae, q. 71, a. 5; Billot, *op. cit.,* pp. 15–20, 37–39.

eternal loss, but which *we desire just the same*. Therefore, even in such sins of omission or of passion we exclude God from our life, we sacrifice Him for a created good, the personal and concrete object of our sin; and this created good, in our dispositions of the moment, becomes truly the dominant love of our heart, the supreme good and end of our life.

II. It may be objected that it is not exactly correct to speak of aversion, of exclusion of God, expressions which imply something absolute and durable, when quite positively the sinner has the sincere desire, the dormant resolve to return to God at least at the end of his life, perhaps even on the next feast day, perhaps by foreseeing and resolving to avoid the next occasion, perhaps even after the present fall which he resolves will be the last. Is it, then, quite exact to speak of aversion and of exclusion of God, when even at the moment of the fall the sinner has in his heart a trace of love for God and regrets displeasing Him?

The sinner wishes to make amends and to return to God because he knows that the enjoyment of sin will not last forever, even in this life and certainly not after death, when he knows eternal punishment is to be avoided. The sinner seems to keep some little love for God since he regrets that he displeases Him. But in reality this love and this regret are merely external, since he offends and sacrifices God just the same. There is even danger that these untrue feelings of regret and love might lead the sinner to a deeper perversion; they might cause him to believe himself more or less excused and authorized by God to mix and confuse the satisfaction of his sensuality with his religious sentimentalism: they consider that to be holy which they themselves desire.

Unless passion totally blinds the sinner, he must recognize that there is no place in his heart for two loves equally dominant and absolute. Love for sin, concretely the love for such or such a good, pleasure, or person, has really supplanted in his heart the love of God. The object of his sin has become his supreme good, his end, his god, which he loves absolutely and completely.

> We cannot serve two masters. . . . The God of the Christians does not wish merely to be loved; He wants to be the one and only object of our love. He does not want us to indulge even in a sigh for anything other than Himself; every other love is a form of idolatry. This exigence is divinely unchangeable. It is impossible to give one's love to the creature without deifying it. It becomes the one thing necessary; it usurps the place of God.[17]

The actual dispositions of the sinner can change. This instability of our impressions, which is a weakness of our nature, can become a force of salvation. The angels, who are pure spirits, became evil by their first fault; our soul, on the contrary, insofar as it is united here below to a body that is mutable in its habits, shares somehow this changeableness. Death alone, if it surprises us, will eternally leave us in the state of sin. Our soul can, therefore, change in this life; and the grace of God is on the alert to profit by any change of dispositions and convert us. But in the dispositions of the moment, the love of the sinner for the concrete and real object of his sin are in themselves absolute and lasting. And if the possibility were offered to him, while he is in these dispositions, to suppress and destroy God, that is to say, to exclude Him forever from his life and destiny, to expect nothing from Him and never to have to fear Him, on condition that he could enjoy his sin forever, he would unhesitatingly profit by this possibility. Therefore, in the actual dispositions of the moment, the object of the passion has replaced God in the heart of the sinner, and has become for

---

[17] François Mauriac, *Souffrances et bonheur du chretien* (Paris, 1931), 26–38.

him his supreme end, his absolute good, his eternal happiness: "He wished to enjoy his sin forever."[18]

III. At any rate, this aversion, or this exclusion of God, does not really touch God Himself. The evil of sin in relation to God belongs exclusively to the intentional order. This evil may be compared, in a sense, to deicide; but it is merely an attempt. St. Thomas repeats this frequently: *"Peccatum non nocet Deo etsi sit contra Deum,"* sin is directed against God, but it does not harm Him.[19]

We surely wish this objection were true. It would be very consoling to think that God is in no way affected by sin. But the very texts of St. Thomas which are presented in favor of the objection make us suspect that there is in sin an evil which in some way reaches God, and which would cause Him to suffer if the Infinite Goodness could suffer; for this evil actually touches Jesus, God's supreme Gift, and Jesus suffered cruelly when He was able to suffer while on earth.

St. Thomas tells us:

> The sinner, by sinning, cannot do God any actual harm: but insofar as he himself is concerned, he acts against God in two ways. First, insofar as he despises God in His commandments. Secondly, insofar as he harms himself or another; which injury redounds upon God, inasmuch as the person injured is an object of God's providence and protection.[20]

It would not be stretching the thought of St. Thomas to present it in this way: Mortal sin does harm to the Increated not in Himself but in the essential order of things desired by Him; hence it does harm Creative Love in His work.

St. Thomas does not go beyond the created order; but he can and should go higher. Unhappily it is not merely Creative

---

[18] St. Augustine, *Epist. 102; P.L.,* L. XXXIII, 381.

[19] St. Thomas, *Summa theol.,* Ia IIae, q. 21, a. 4, ad 1; q. 47, a. 1, ad 1.

[20] St. Thomas, *Summa theol.,* Ia Iae, q. 47, a. 1, ad 1.

Love, it is the Sanctifying Love which is harmed by sin, harmed in His most magnificent work, the gift, the life of Jesus in us. God really counts and exists for us in His gifts which constitute His work and all of which center in Jesus. The Father has eternally predestined us in Christ; through the incarnation and death of Jesus He has saved us, has adopted us as His children, has sanctified us. We should go further and see how the Father identifies these gifts with Jesus, how they are for Him something of Jesus living in us. For in reality all the gifts of grace and love which exist in our soul, all the beauty and consecration which the character of sonship gives us, belong more to Christ than to ourselves. It is His life in us; it is the extension of His Mystical Body; it is the increase of glory and joy which He offers to His Father in heaven and in the Host.

All this is affected and destroyed by mortal sin. Our eternal election is checkmated and lost; the gift of the incarnation becomes a terrible condemnation if we die in our sin; our incorporation to Christ survives in a character without beauty and without rights; and the life of Christ in us, the life of grace dies completely. Yes, God is affected by mortal sin, affected in His loving work of our sanctification, affected in the life of Jesus, His well-beloved Son, in our soul.

And Jesus Himself would suffer again, if He could, since His life, character, and mission of love for the Father and for souls is so directly affected by sin. He felt the evil of our sins throughout His earthly life, when He was able to suffer; this was particularly so in the agony at Gethsemani when anguish pierced His heart at the sight, so hideous and sad, of the sins of mankind. *Delicta quis intelligit?* Who can understand sin? There is in sin an unfathomable mystery, a mystery of power, but of power for evil, against God and against Jesus. Heart of Jesus, Victim for sin, have mercy on us!

Chapter IV ✤ The Time for Conversion

THE PURGATIVE RETREAT OF THE NOVITIATE

DIVINE mercy is not limited by time or place. The light of conversion may shine for a soul at any time and in the most diverse circumstances. God waits for some souls until the end of their long and foolish life of sin, as the father in the parable waited for years for the return of his prodigal son. To other souls God offers early graces for their conversion and, at the time of their First Communion, gives them a true spiritual life, sufficiently and solidly established because it rests on humility and confidence.

To others already converted and striving for many years to advance in virtue, God may again bestow at a given moment the graces of the purgative way, especially if they are to be promoted to some eminent dignity and need to feel their lowliness that they may avoid the intoxication of their elevation. Long ago, St. Gregory the Great bore witness to this fact:

> Those whom God wishes to raise to sanctity by promoting them to some high dignity need very much to be strengthened against the fascination and freedom of power. The grace of humility will scatter the clouds of vain glory, will guard them from boastful speech, will save them from the turmoil and errors of purely natural action.[1]

Why does God suddenly seem to desire that a soul, already as far as the higher ways of mysticism, should retrace its steps along the lower path of the purification of the senses and of the heart? Simply to make it more humble and more

---

[1] St. Gregory the Great, *Moralia,* V, 2.

pure by making it realize the sadness and evil of sin, to make it share more intimately in His agony and to continue to be through it "the man of sorrows and acquainted with infirmity . . . whom the Lord was pleased to bruise in infirmity."[2]

Yes, the ways of the light of conversion remain as mysterious to us as the other ways of the divine wisdom and love. However, there is a singularly propitious time, during which God seems to delight in bestowing upon souls the treasures of His light of purity and strength. It is the time of the novitiate, particularly the days of the purgative retreat.

The custom in some religious institutes is to begin the novitiate with the complete *Spiritual Exercises* of St. Ignatius. The rest of the canonical time is spent by the novices in realizing the logical consequences of the choice of a life of perfection. Other institutes — and we favor this practice — distribute the four weeks of the *Spiritual Exercises* throughout the course of the novitiate. Thus these weeks are a vital force which develops gradually during this blessed year. Each retreat is prepared by the conferences of the master of novices and by the personal efforts of the novices themselves. In this way the final aim of the novitiate seems to be attained more surely: the aspirant to the religious life is led forward along the purgative and even the illuminative way. We shall treat exclusively of the purgative retreat. It will be easy to show the dynamic power of this retreat to effect true conversion.

I. The Meditations of the Purgative Retreat

Usually these meditations are borrowed from the *Spiritual Exercises* of St. Ignatius. Other accepted manuals of retreats are generally popular presentations of the *Exercises*. This wonderful work has served as basis to subsequent authors, it has

---

[2] Isa. 53:3, 10.

condensed the teachings of ancient masters, it maintains throughout a true spiritual tone. The aim of the *Exercises* is to purify the soul in order to persuade it to lead a true Christian life. Their very title suggests this: "Spiritual Exercises, chosen with the aim of assisting a man in the conquest of self, so that after liberating himself from the fatal influence of evil attachments, he may fix upon a plan for a truly Christian life."

The first week of the *Exercises* is particularly directed along the lines of the purgative life. The meditations begin with what St. Ignatius and all other authors call the Foundation, that is, the consideration of this truth: my whole being, all that I am and have, and whatever surrounds me to help me and to serve me, come wholly *from* God: therefore all belong wholly *to* God and are wholly *for* God. In prayer, we dwell upon this truth until we realize our condition as creatures, our state of absolute dependence upon God, His complete power over us, our nothingness and His all. This is followed by a series of meditations on sin, its malice and consequences, seen chiefly at the moment of death and judgment, seen in the eternal duration of hell when our aversion from God turns against us and becomes our eternal malediction. They last for ten days, and with the help of prayer will normally lead us to feel the evil of sin, to be truly sorry for it, and take practical steps to amend our lives. At the same time, they will cause us to make the resolution to do anything, to suffer anything rather than commit mortal sin in the future.

St. Ignatius held to the order of these meditations, but left to the director of the exercises the liberty to add other subjects, provided they were in line with these fundamental truths. However, the closest followers of St. Ignatius introduce in the last days of the first week subjects that are more related to the love of God and of our Lord. Thus, Petitdidier presents on the last two days meditations on contrition through love,

on the prodigal son as a motive and model of conversion,
on the invitation of Christ to follow Him, on the Eucharist
as the complement of our reconciliation and the food of our
new life.[3]

The fundamental meditations, indeed, gain in force of conviction and grace of attraction if Jesus, our Saviour has in
them His proper place. Everything in these meditations
tends to recall His thoughts, His presence, His actions. The
rights of God over us, His rights as our Father, are rights
based on love; and God is our Father in Jesus. To see how
much we are of God, that is to say, how much we have
received from Him, we must see Him in Jesus Christ Himself: our election in Christ, our incorporation to His filiation
and His life of grace. To see how much we belong to God
and are destined for God, we must see how much Christ is
God's and for God: ". . . for all are yours, and you are
Christ's, and Christ is God's."[4] To see all the evil of mortal
sin we must see that sin touches God in the reality of His
gifts to our soul, in the very life of Jesus in us.

We constantly mention prayer as the soul of our meditations, for prayer is indispensable to obtain the light of conversion of heart, the gifts of intelligence, wisdom, and counsel.
And if it is true that Jesus must have an essential part in
our fundamental meditations, it is also very true that He must
have a part in the prayer that fructifies these meditations.
Formerly, when the novices were asked to abstain from
receiving Holy Communion during the ten days of the purgative retreat, Jesus seemed far away and absent. This privation,
imposed by the rule and by tradition, was accepted as the
will of God; but it was keenly felt during those interminable
ten days. Today it lasts only until the general confession,
that is, for about five days. We should like to see this present

---

[3] Petitdidier, S.J., *Exercitia spiritualia* (Lyons, 1834), pp. 100–113.
[4] 1 Cor. 3:23.

custom continued. Realizing its sins, the soul "cuts itself off," and finds great graces of light, humility, and penance in this attitude of the poor publican who stood afar off, striking his breast, and not daring to lift up his eyes, but whom God saw and justified. This separation will end in a more loving and more fervent Communion. But, from the very start of the exercises, the director must be careful to arouse great confidence in the hearts of the novices and to keep them united with Jesus, their Saviour.

II. *The Examination of Conscience During the Purgative Retreat*

This examination has a twofold aim: to prepare us for a general confession of our entire life and to set in order the background of our resolutions for the future. Canon Law prescribes a general confession before entrance into the novitiate, that is, at the end of the postulantship, if this preliminary step is required: Postulants, before they begin their novitiate, will devote at least eight full days to spiritual exercises; and, in accordance with the prudent judgment of their confessor, will make a general confession of their past life.[5] Since it leaves it to the prudent judgment of the confessor, the Code evidently does not wish to impose strictly a general confession before the novitiate. Yet some commentators insist that even in institutes where there is no formal postulantship prescribed it would be better to make a general confession before entrance or very shortly after the beginning of the novitiate. We like to believe that if the confessor of the postulants is free to judge the appropriate time for a general confession, the confessor appointed for the novitiate and the master of the novices should enjoy a similar privilege. Commonly the general confession is postponed until the purgative retreat which

---

[5] *Codex Juris Canonici,* 541.

takes place seven or eight weeks after the beginning of the novitiate.

Happily it is only in rare cases that a general confession of one's whole life is strictly necessary as the prelude to a true conversion. Ordinarily it remains simply a useful aid in the work of conversion. A general confession of one's whole life or of a part thereof is absolutely necessary when a novice is certain that during most of his life or for some period at least his confessions have been invalid or sacrilegious, usually because they have been incomplete. As a child he did not confess everything; he did not dare to confess everything. He voluntarily kept back some sin which he knew was grave at the time it was committed; or he did not reveal some serious circumstances that altered the nature of the sin. Again, there is need for a general confession if as a child the novice did not have the required contrition or purpose of amendment, even though the confessions themselves were complete. This case is not as clear as the preceding one, unless there is question of mortal sins that have been accused without the desire and wish to avoid future voluntary occasions of sin.

Outside of these cases of necessity, there is no absolute obligation to make a general confession. It is, however, very useful and it is recommended very strongly to the novices during the purgative retreat. It may be useful and advisable even for a soul who was told in the world by his confessor never to confess again sins that were already forgiven. This confessor may not have anticipated a religious vocation and the special graces of the novitiate. A general confession is among the special graces given to novices because it makes them realize better the number and the gravity of their sins, it purifies them more completely through a more humble and a more trusting confession, or it leads them to a deeper gratitude toward the Divine Love who chose them despite so many infidelities and to a more ardent desire for expiation.

The review of his past life will aid the novice in knowing himself better, and thus in preparing for his life in the future. He will ask himself the following questions:

What have been the occasions or the circumstances that have contributed most to my falls into sin?

What were the moral or the psychological consequences of these sins? Perhaps I was discouraged or irritated because my self-love was wounded. Or I may have become indifferent, and as a result my subsequent confessions were bad, and my evil inclinations became more deeply rooted. Or perhaps the result was genuine and prompt sorrow followed by a good confession, a more fervent Communion, and a more sincere effort to atone for these faults.

What does my past life reveal concerning my character, my temperament, my good or evil inclinations, and especially my dominant fault: for that is the ever vulnerable spot in my soul, the breach through which mortal sin might again enter into my life?

The answers to these questions will help the novice to determine more precisely the lines along which he should carry his resolute fight and constant effort to persevere in true conversion of heart and to advance in the life of union with our Lord.

Chapter V ❧ Two Extremes That Should Be Avoided in Our Reaction Against Past Sins

FACED with his sinful past the beginner, in his eagerness to purify himself, is exposed to the danger of falling into either of two extremes which may destroy his spiritual fervor and even at times do serious harm to his physical health. These two extremes are, on the one hand, an untimely and dangerous reflection on his past sins, and, on the other, indiscreet mortifications.

I. Untimely and Dangerous Reflection on Past Sins

Before daring to think of my sins I must first try to lift up my soul to God, to live in the white light of His sanctity. To grope among the sins and miseries of the past may be dangerous in some states of the soul. It may be a fresh temptation. . . . Yes, before every examination of conscience, before every retrospect, before every glance backwards towards the past, it is well to lift up our souls to God, to place ourselves in His presence, to look upwards. There is a cavern in Southern Italy, in which poisonous vapours cling to the ground, as the guides prove for the traveller by flinging in dogs which instantly become insensible, and would perish, if not dragged out at once, while men are safe as long as they hold themselves erect. To grope and grovel amidst the sinful past, is perilous in like manner; we must stand upright; we must lift up our souls to God.[1]

We should always be on the alert against unhealthy visions of the past, even when we do not voluntarily turn

---

[1] Russell, S.J., *At Home With God* (New York: Longmans, Green, 1910).

61

our thoughts to them. The recurring and troublesome impressions of our sins are explained very naturally by the images that are still imprinted on our mind, by the persevering bent of our former habits, by sparks of affection that have not been entirely extinguished in our heart. What would then be the result if we were to examine our faults minutely and stir up the muddy bottom of our past without first protecting ourselves by a vigorous and decisive movement of our soul toward God? We would be encompassed by a noxious and deathly atmosphere!

Usually at the beginning of conversion the soul is still too near its sin; it has not yet sufficiently absorbed the purifying light from above to be able to examine with impunity the details of its past life.

> Beginners are to be cautioned against a distinct consideration of each sin . . . and even against recalling their former life because in the first stages of conversion there is danger, as a rule, lest the images of past indiscretions excite an unsteady mind.[2]

The only time in our life when we are able to examine without danger our whole past, and to count and measure our faults, is in the supernatural atmosphere of the purgative retreat, when our meditations on God, His rights and His love, have lifted up our soul to the serene regions of divine light and of infinite sanctity. Let us not be afraid, for at that time in the presence of God we see our sins as He Himself sees them. There, in the presence of His infinite justice and holiness, the sight of our sins will only arouse in us the hatred of evil, something of the hatred that God Himself experiences, something of the deep and mysterious loathing, something of the deathly sadness of Christ, when He lay

---

[2] LeGaudier, *op. cit.*, p. 176.

prostrated and crushed under the weight of the sins of the world in the agony at Gethsemani.

Outside of this singular time, the converted soul will not have the need nor the right to recall in detail each of its past faults. Undoubtedly, after this period of extraordinary purification the soul, no matter how high it may rise, will never forget that in the past it has sinned. This knowledge will help the soul to become more humble as it realizes how guilty it has been with regard to God and to Jesus; to recognize and exalt all the more God's infinite mercy with regard to its almost infinite misery; and, finally, to purify itself still more from all the iniquity of its past life by placing it entirely under the blood of Jesus at each confession: *Amplius lava me ab iniquitate mea.* Just a general thought over past sins will suffice to produce these blessed fruits, especially since the soul is aided more each time by the light of faith and of love.

II. *Indiscreet Mortifications*

Excesses in mortification are to be guarded against, chiefly because they have the appearance of a logical outgrowth of true conversion. Hatred for sin and contemplation of the cross seem to lead thither almost by necessity both the guilty soul who feels the need to avenge God against himself and the soul who has remained pure from youth but who wants just the same to punish his body to keep it in subjection, who is anxious to carry the weight of the sins of the world in the footsteps of the Lamb. It is love that goes the limit: something, surely, to be admired.

But is it possible that excess is truly inspired by love? Prudence is inseparable from the gift of divine charity: "Love for God is most prudent and never acts indiscreetly."[3] God

---

[3] *Ibid.,* p. 177.

cannot approve indiscretions, much less inspire them. His grace moves us to live in obedience; Jesus recognizes our love by this virtue. Now, obedience to our rules, to our superiors, to our confessor, would prevent indiscretion. Therefore, let us not be deceived. Let us not look to God, but to our own nature and at times to the wiles of the devil for the inspiration of our unwise mortifications.

Nature does not die with conversion. It never dies. That is why it mixes, at times, vanity with the first fervor of the converted soul and makes it feel a need to distinguish itself in mortification, by striving to do more than others. This is why, on rare occasions, it leads certain nervous temperaments by some remains of morbid sensuality to corporal tortures which are as dangerous to modesty as they are to health.

Ordinarily the influence of nature shows itself in the succession of feelings and impressions which make up, or at least guide, the life of many beginners. Before their conversion, they were prey to their impressions; they remain so after they are converted. No doubt, sentiments of piety and zeal have supplanted their former worldly and sinful sentiments. But basically, now as formerly, the soul is the toy and the slave of these impressions. An impulsive young man who was yesterday impelled to evil almost in spite of himself, today remains impulsive and lets himself be led to excessive penances. Questioned, he would answer now as he did before, in the face of his evil inclinations: "I am made like that." "All or nothing." "I can't help it; this thing is stronger than I am." Grace, no doubt, makes use of our impressions to convert us. As we already remarked, this very changeability of sentiments renders us capable of being converted, whereas the pure spirits remained unchanged after their first fall. Grace, as it makes use of our impressions, should purify and dominate them; that is to say, it should subject them forever to the dictates of reason and faith. But, alas, they are neither purified nor dominated if they continue to motivate our life after conversion. The excesses of today can well cause us to fear a return to the impressions of yesterday.

The devil himself may play a part in these excesses. He knows to perfection the changing character of our impressions and can deftly play on our impulsive temperament, so full of imaginations and feelings, to make us start too fast, then to stop us, and finally to mislead us on our way toward perfection. How frequently a period of excessive fervor and of imprudent penances ends in the ruin of an already fragile nervous system, in weariness and discouragement, and perhaps in the total abandonment of one's efforts!

The devil fears fasting, since he was driven away by it. Our Lord assures us of this in the advice He gave the Apostles after the cure of the unfortunate child possessed by the devil. But He means fasting united to prayer, that is, the spirit of sacrifice united to the spirit of humility.[4] Abstinences and mortifications without interior renunciation serve only the purpose of the evil one.

Nowadays, especially, when the personality of the individual with its daring ideas and feelings is accentuated in proportion to the highly nervous tension of the person's temperament, corporal mortification is less needed, perhaps even less possible than in the days of our forefathers, who were of sturdier health and so calm in action and repose. On the other hand, however, now more than ever the evangelical law of total renunciation, the renunciation of heart, will, and mind, is particularly imperative.

To sum up, a "beginner" who is truly converted should feel the pressing need, even the attraction of mortification. It is the sign that he detests sin and is willing to make amends. But prudence and obedience should always rule his

---

[4] Mt. 17:20; Mk. 9:28.

corporal penances. On the other hand, there is no limit as regards interior renunciation; for the more the soul crucifies itself with its evil tendencies and desires, the more it will live in Christ Jesus.[5]

One last remark. We are speaking here of "beginners" and for "beginners." Our cautions can, however, apply also to those advancing on the illuminative way. But souls who have arrived at the third stage may be drawn by the grace of perfect union to mortifications outside the common rules of prudence and discretion. It is for their director to discern the origin of them. If he is confident that it is the Spirit of Jesus who leads them, he should abandon them to His guidance. The life of Father Ginhac offers us a typical case of excessive mortifications authorized by the director and tolerated by the superiors. Father Lallemant formulates the golden rule in this manner:

> The middle course that should be followed with regard to penances is not to overdo them because one's health would suffer, and not to minimize them to such an extent as to let nature get the upper hand. Once a soul arrives at a high degree of perfection, they come rather easily; and through a special favor of God they may even be heroic, after the manner of the saints, and not be injurious to health. The most hurtful are those which take away sleep, although God grants to perfect souls the grace of sleeping very little. Therefore, the measure of penance differs according to individuals, their constitution, times, and needs.[6]

---

[5] Gal. 2:19 f.
[6] Lallemant, *op. cit.*, Part 2, p. 69.

Chapter VI   Scruples, a Frequent Danger on the Road to Conversion

A SCRUPLE is a fear of sin which disturbs the soul but has no foundation. It is not a judgment or conviction of the mind that is based on fact or solid reasoning; it is an erroneous impression of the imagination that besieges and harasses the soul; it is a species of obsession or of phobia.

In an answer given on May 28, 1915, by the Sacred Congregation of the Sacraments on a case of doubt concerning intention in ordination to the priesthood, an answer which fills more than four pages in the *Acta Apostolicae Sedis,* we find the clearest and best authorized theory concerning scruples in general.

> The scruple properly so called does not reside in the intellect, nor in the will, nor in the conscience; it resides only in the imagination. Hence, when the imagination is troubled, the scrupulous person mistakes for the true voice of conscience, for a true decision, for real consent, what in reality is merely a judgment, a decision, a consent of the imagination. . . . The great fear or phobia of committing sin upsets the imagination of the scrupulous person, and he is no longer capable of placing a deliberate and free act, in that condition of mind. Hence, under the influence of the scruple, all succeeding movements of his mind are effects of the imagination, and outside the imagination have neither value nor force.[1]

We do not purpose to give a complete treatise on scruples; it will be sufficient to describe the ordinary form, the cause,

---

[1] *Acta Apostolicae Sedis* (1915), 411–415, esp. 414.

and the remedy of this sickness, insofar as it may frequently attack the soul in her efforts along the purgative way.[2]

The Ordinary Form of Scruples During the Period of Conversion

Scrupulous fear may bear on past sins or on present temptations. We distinguish the two cases, remembering, however, that they often unite to torment the soul of the beginner. With regard to past sins, the unhappy beginner is constantly tormented by the distressing thought that he has surely committed some particular sin and that he has never confessed it; or at least that he has never completely and clearly explained it in all its particular circumstances; that, most of the time, he has lacked sufficient contrition, and that, in some cases at least, he surely did not have it.

He does not have a shadow of reason to support these fears; they are pure imaginations, with no foundation whatsoever. Yet, these fears attack his soul, take possession of it and torment it. Under their influence, the scrupulous person multiplies his examinations of conscience, his minute and interminable accusations, which at times are even unbecoming. But all his efforts are wasted; for after each attempt finally to make a "good confession" the obsession returns with the same force and the same grief.

With regard to present temptations, the unhappy youth sees a mortal sin in every thought, imagination, or impression against faith, chastity, charity. He is radically incapable of distinguishing between a simple suggestion of the mind (a thought or an image that possesses a certain natural attraction) and the consent of the will itself. By reason, indeed, of the psychological automatism that constitutes the scrupulous

---

[2] Cf. Eymieu, S.J., *Le gouvernement de soi-meme,* 2ᵉ volume: *L'obsession et le scrupule.* Gemelli, O.F.M., *De scrupulis.*

obsession, a simple suggestion or imagination of evil awakens and forces the impression of consent already given. Hardly has the consciousness of a temptation appeared than the scrupulous person hears as an inevitable reaction an interior voice that tells him: "Too late to resist; you have consented. The sin has been committed. . . ." There is no semblance of truth in this so-called voice of conscience. Free will has really nothing to do with this irresistible stream of linked and haunting impressions. But the soul is blindly mistaken; it feels, it sees sin everywhere.

The Causes of These Scruples

The first cause of scruples generally lies in the temperament and character of the newly converted person. We may have noticed that almost always a scrupulous person is one of those anemic temperaments, inclined to melancholy, which present a fertile ground for deep and persistent emotions of fear, sadness, pessimism. A scruple, as a matter of fact, is nothing but a particular form of these somber and depressing emotions, a "phobia" which complicates and confuses the problems of conscience.

Recourse to a reliable doctor may remedy in part this constitutional tendency to melancholy and scruples.[3] If a doctor is not consulted, a great deal of attention should be given to the temperament and the health of the subject inclined to scruples. This is essentially true during certain periods when the subject must, so to speak, follow his conscience more closely and examine his moral life more minutely. This occurs chiefly during the novitiate. Fatigue will result if no attention is given to the health, that is, to the food, sleep, and relaxation of a young man who is very active, of a quick mind, very generous and prone to overdo his mortifica-

---

[3] Gemelli, *op. cit.,* pp. 259–263.

tions. Nervous excitement and his natural vivacity will unite to cause him, while he reviews his past life and examines his present condition, to find the most disconcerting things about the motives and consequences of his faults, defects in his confessions, and the most farfetched possibilities of consent in regard to actual temptations. His findings will become a veritable torture to his soul and will increase his anemia and his nervousness.

The devil can also intervene in scruples. He can succeed in whispering vain and somber apprehensions even to the clearest and best balanced minds. Still more easily can he turn any form of nervousness or melancholy into a real scruple. His action is veiled under the interplay of our own faculties and natural tendencies but it is nevertheless to be feared. His purpose is to stop the beginner, to draw him back, or at least to slacken his pace on the road to conversion and progress.

The results of these scrupulous crises in which the devil has a share may be disastrous. The soul may grow discouraged and indifferent, finding piety insipid and the yoke of the Lord unbearable. Or it may lose the taste and joy of perfection seeing itself doomed to lead a sad existence along a miry road, in an atmosphere of morbid impressions. Or, finally, it may become blindly and incurably selfish, because, at the basis of any scruple, there exists not an exaggerated love for God and a fear to displease Him, but an exasperated seeking for our own security, our own peace and satisfaction in the service of God. Some have identified the selfishness of the scruple with hysterical egotism. This is expressing it too strongly, but the two do have points in common which give satisfaction to the enemy of the love of God in our soul.

At times God Himself may submit the beginner to the test of the scruple. God may, as a matter of fact, withdraw for a time the graces which permit the beginner to see clearly his past life, and to distinguish between impression and consent in actual temptations. Men like St. Ignatius of Loyola, St. Francis de Sales, St. Alphonsus of Liguori experienced this providential trial. In this case, as we said, the crisis is of short duration. Instead of ending in discouragement and laxness, it aids the work of conversion and progress. It purifies the soul more delicately by plunging it into a deeper humility, by inspiring it to distrust and be detached from the most precious of its natural qualities, the acuteness of its mind and the sureness of its judgment.

The Remedy for These Scruples

Let us, first, forestall the use of two remedies which the scrupulous person eagerly seeks, because they are illusory and even render matters worse.

The first false remedy is opening one's conscience "completely and for the last time" to an enlightened director and hoping for an answer that is "convincing and definitive." The scrupulous person is constantly seeking a director that will enlighten him and finally give him peace. How frequently he has tried to describe perfectly his case to a director, hoping for a clear-cut, direct, and convincing answer! Each time he felt sure he had found the desired guide; each time he hoped and thought that this new director who listened to him patiently, who questioned him, counseled him at great length, had understood his doubts, had dispelled them for good, and calmed all his anxieties. Alas, soon he again found himself questioning the reasons his director had given him; again the same doubts, the same questions, the same obscurities invaded his soul and tormented him with even greater force.

In reality he is not cured, and he will not be cured if he continues this method of giving minute explanations on his part, and seeking more logical and wiser explanations from his director. These remedies belong to the realm of facts and reason, and his sickness is in his impressions. They are like two parallel lines which will never join.

These illustrations may help to bring out our point. We can suppose the case of a man who at the moment of retiring is afraid because he remembers seeing a suspicious character lurking around the neighborhood that evening. And we can also imagine the case of a child who, when his mother puts out the light at night and leaves the room, is afraid to go to sleep in the darkness. The man would rise, would check the doors and windows where the thief might enter, would inspect the corners and places where he might be hidden; and upon discovering that there is nothing amiss would go to sleep in peace. This is an image of the penitent with the right and firm spirit, who has examined his conscience carefully, has seen and spoken clearly, and, trusting his director, continues his work in peace. Here, on the other hand, is the picture of the scrupulous person: he is the child who is afraid of darkness and cries, calling for his mother. She comes, puts on the light, shows him that there is no one hidden in the room, that no one can hide there and leaves him smiling and reassured. But only for a minute, as long as the impression of her caress remains. And if he does not go to sleep immediately under that impression, he will again be afraid, and once again will cry for help. This is exactly the case of the scrupulous soul. After his last talk with the director, due to the latter's kindness and patience in listening and counseling him, he has a moment of respite and of calm. But this goodness, this encouragement, these consolations which he received are unable to supplant the changing sensibility of his nature. And the most convincing reasons fail because they cannot reach the impressions; since all the evil comes from these impressions, the scruples will remain. As a matter of fact, the good impression caused by the new director will quickly disappear and the agonizing obsessions will again reign supreme.

The second false remedy is a new and complete confession of past faults that will at last be satisfactory. The scrupulous person is sure that he would finally attain lasting peace of mind if he were allowed to make a new general confession. Yes, this would really be the last one! And he anxiously seeks to make this new general confession a good one, either to his ordinary confessor, or, better still, to another confessor.

But this remedy, were he allowed to use it, would only render his condition worse. We grant that his soul would be calm for a few hours, even for a few days. Soon, however, this new confession, which at first seemed so soothing, would beget new questionings! "Did I accuse myself of such or such a thing" . . . "Was I explicit enough on such or such a point?" . . . and so on *ad infinitum*. And after these questionings comes the doubt, and after the doubts the same anxiety, or rather a more painful anxiety because the soul feels more abandoned and lonely. The following comparison is rather striking, although not very lofty: just as the insides of a person given to drink are temporarily soothed by each potion which stimulates him for a moment, and yet burns and harms him all the more, in like manner each new accusation eases for a moment the torment of the poor scrupulous person only to agonize him more painfully later on.

What, then, is the one effective remedy? It is an absolute and blind obedience to the confessor on the subject matter of the scruples. The scrupulous person should pray to God to obtain the grace of finding a director that is able to see clearly and speak firmly, a director or confessor who inspires confidence and demands obedience. This confidence will be based on the fitness and the goodness of the director, who should be a true spiritual father. The obedience will be based on the absolute authority of God Himself; and the director should never consent to give reasons or admit any discussion. Above all, he should not reverse his opinion.[4]

Even when his conscience tells the scrupulous person that he has surely committed a certain sin, that he has never confessed it, that he has surely consented to a certain temptation, even when he feels ready to swear that he is guilty, gravely guilty, yes, even then, he has the right and duty to ignore this voice of his conscience, or rather of his imagination, and to follow blindly the guidance of his confessor who orders him to overlook all his fears and to receive Holy Communion in spite of it all.

What principle of theology justifies such a rigorous and absolute rule? Ordinarily this saving principle is presented to the scrupulous soul in this manner: On the particular field of your scruples, your conscience is essentially mistaken and, therefore, does not have any longer before God the mission or the right to judge your actions and to direct your life. On this field, the duty to direct you has been entrusted by God Himself to your confessor or director. You must, in the name

---

[4] Cf. especially Eymieu, *op. cit.,* pp. 220–237.

Gemelli (*op. cit.,* pp. 268–293, esp. p. 291) speaking directly to confessors, summarizes this doctrine in the following way: "A command to a scrupulous person must be so phrased as to exclude all doubt with regard to its meaning. The scrupulous person will, indeed, find ambiguity where there is none. But woe if the confessor or doctor uses words that are wanting in precision and clarity! Still worse would it be to use the word *perhaps.* The command should be given decisively and absolutely, unaccompanied by justifying reasons. Any attempt at justification engenders doubts. Note further that it is not enough to give a command. While the confessor or doctor is talking, the mind of the penitent or patient wanders far afield and is attentive only to its own ruminations. We must make sure that he hears and understands the formula of the command we give him. It may be necessary to repeat it several times and to insist upon it.

of this divine Authority, obey your confessor, and obey him blindly in anything that concerns your scruples.[5]

Is this the happiest manner of presenting this principle? Does it best answer the nature and the psychology of scruples, the analysis of their consequences, the respect due to the human personality, liberty, and conscience? True, scruples sometimes unbalance a person, both physically and mentally, to such an extent that we can truthfully speak of a thorough aberration, and even of surrender of conscience. These cases, however, are extreme and exceptional. So, in order to justify blind obedience to the confessor on the part of the scrupulous person, we prefer to use another formula better suited to the normal or more common form of scruples, one that seems more in line with the psychological explanation of this mental malady and which at the same time respects better the dignity of the human conscience.

We would say to the scrupulous person: With regard to your scruples, this voice that keenly troubles you is only the voice of your overexcited imagination, which assumes wrongfully the role of your conscience. The frantic impressions caused by the vision of imaginary sins deaden at present the voice of your true conscience. In previous and calmer moments, however, when you were able to hear it, the voice of your true conscience spoke distinctly; it still speaks even though you are unable to hear it amid the tumult of your imaginary impressions. It used to tell you and tells you over again: In periods of crisis and of total bewilderment you should have recourse to the guide that God has given you in the person of the confessor, and you should obey him blindly in order to despise your scruples, for this guide can make

---

[5] Eymieu, *op. cit.,* pp. 238–239, 246–284. The answer of the Sacred Congregation of the Sacraments mentioned above seems to speak in the same tone: "In this upset state the scrupulous person is no longer capable of a deliberate will," that is of a truly free, human act.

you hear my voice, the voice of right reason and truth, not the deceitful voice of impressions and feelings.

However, let us not forget that the principle of blind obedience to the confessor retains its full validity as the essential remedy for scruples, whatever may be the formula of its justification. If the unhappy, scrupulous person were to refuse this unique remedy, he would endanger his spiritual progress, perhaps even his perseverance on the road of true conversion, not to mention his physical and mental health. If he accepts it, he will be cured.

The cure will not be instantaneous, for the struggle of impressions against right reason may still last for a while. The scrupulous person may even go through moments more particularly painful, when he fears he has deceived his confessor, when he has the feeling of being in mortal sin and even of having made a sacrilegious Communion, when he feels, as it were, doomed to die in this frightening situation. But if he perseveres in his faith and trust in Jesus and in His priest; if, in the midst of this more bitter crisis, he continues to pray and to approach the holy table, sooner or later, at the time chosen by Divine Wisdom and Love, his obedience will bring him victory.

And while he waits, this trial, hard as it is, will purify him all the more from any attachment to self; and his communion to the agony of the Saviour will prepare him the more perfectly for the heights of the second and third stages of the spiritual life.

Chapter VII ✻ Willful Temptations,

Obstacle to a Lasting Conversion

How can a soul that is truly converted fall again into mortal sin? Is it not firmly established in an attitude of stern opposition to sin? Is it not, therefore, a seeming contradiction to speak of a converted soul that lets itself fall into mortal sin? All this is true. If the soul remained firm in its conversion, if mortal sin appeared to it openly, it would shrink from it and reject it with horror. As long as the soul remains attached to God, its last end, its only good, as long as it loves Him with all its heart, the soul will not become attached to a created good that will suddenly turn it away from God.

Unfortunately mortal sin does not present itself suddenly and openly to the soul that is truly converted and that wishes to remain so forever. Rather it hides itself under the snare of willful temptations and creeps in through the long detours of lukewarmness. Such a soul would rather die than commit a single mortal sin. It is sincere. But it may also wish to dally with the snare of the temptation, feeling sure that the danger is not grave or that it will be able at least to stop in time. It may also wish to find a little satisfaction in some particular venial sin which would cost it too much to give up, telling itself of its resolution never to cross the line which separates this venial sin from mortal sin. And thus, misled by its presumption and urged on by latent vestiges of attraction for the object of mortal sin, the converted soul ends by sacrificing the principle of true conversion. Its absolute opposition to mortal sin weakens little by little; it is gradually led to consider, to taste, and to conceive a growing affection for the object of that sin, until the moment arrives when this love becomes dominant and takes the place of God in its heart; the moment, consequently, when mortal sin is committed: "A turning away from God our last end through affection for a creature good." This is the way, the only way that can lead a truly converted soul to mortal sin: either playing with temptation or deciding in its own favor the attitude to take concerning a particular venial sin or lukewarmness.

Playing with temptation comes quite often very close to lukewarmness. Perhaps it is better to say that lukewarmness always includes such dangerous playing. However, lukewarmness goes further. A soul can, without being lukewarm, be led into mortal sin by entering into temptation once in passing. Tepidity supposes persistence in the dangerous dallying which causes us to enter into temptation; it supposes that a person has assumed a deliberate bent toward venial sin, even in the matter of his dominant fault. As a result, it gives rise to a more or less hidden disorganization of the spiritual life and should be feared much more than a mere accidental fall. The difference between the passing fall which may result from a presumptuous entrance into temptation and falls due to tepidity is best illustrated by the comparison between a serious but accidental sickness, clearly diagnosed and defined, which can be cured easily and promptly, and a lingering malady which having long undermined the system, manifests itself only when it is too late. Authors also compare the fall of St. Peter with the fall of Judas to illustrate the difference between grave sin which results from an accidental imprudence and the fatal consequences brought about by lukewarmness. We shall, therefore, consider separately this twofold danger: temptations and lukewarmness.

In regard to temptations a distinction must be made. We know that here below temptations are inevitable. The words of the *Imitation of Christ* are well known:

As long as we live in this world, we cannot be without tribulation and temptation. . . . No one is so perfect and holy as not sometimes to have temptations. . . . There is no order so holy, nor place so retired, where there are no temptations.

And the author explains this general law of temptation with the following reason: "A man is never wholly secure from temptation as long as he lives; for there is within us the source of temptation."[1] The devil also has a share in temptations. The author of the *Imitation* certainly did not ignore the advice of St. Peter: "Be sober and watch well: because your adversary the devil, as a roaring lion, goeth about seeking whom he may devour."[2] Thus, it happens at times that very humble and pure souls are so tempted by pride and impurity that we cannot but recognize the intervention of the agent of revolt and corruption. However, we need not necessarily appeal to the malice of the devil to explain our temptations. We should be careful, very careful, before explaining them by his direct intervention. Timid souls and children may be frightened and obsessed by the terror of this enemy. Other simple but weak souls blame the power and malice of the devil for all their falls: "The devil got the best of Johnny," a jovial old Irish gardener used to tell us as an excuse for his frequent visits to the saloon.

There is within us the source of temptation. This is the word that we should constantly keep in mind. Our nature molded out of the earth's dust and of light, our body dragging us down, our mind rising too high in its pride, constitute the primary source of our temptations. Temptation is the necessary consequence of our nature; it is also the indispensable condition of our strength and our progress in the spiritual order. It is the test of our moral value; he who has not been tempted,

[1] *Imitation of Christ*, Book I, Chap. 13.

[2] 1 Pet. 5:8.

what does he know and what can he do? Later on, we shall enumerate the benefits of this trial, showing how, in the actual plan of Providence, temptation is one of the most effective instruments of our crucifixion with Christ, so that we may live more and more the life of Christ. The converted soul is not to be denied this blessed trial. On the one hand, its conversion has not freed it from the weight of the body of this death and, on the other hand, the converted soul is committed to an effort to rise higher in its union with Christ by the crucifixion of all its vicious tendencies and desires.

Temptation, therefore, is a necessary consequence of our nature and an indispensable test in the providential plan of our sanctification. Would that it were only this! Unfortunately, it is also a danger. More so for the beginner, for the newly converted soul. It may discourage him, or make him presumptuous. For he might, when faced by a temptation that he has not sought, that he has even feared too much, that attacks him, as it were, despite himself — he might, due to a lack of humility and confidence, think himself too weak, and he might yield through discouragement, obsessed by a feeling of defeat. Or again, thinking himself too strong and immune to mortal sin by the fact of his conversion, the beginner might refuse to suspect the trap and the danger hidden in the lingering vestiges of attachment for some good, some pleasure, some affection which formerly constituted for him an object of sin. He may desire to play again with the snare, resolved and sure that he will never again be caught. In this presumption he is almost unconsciously walking toward a fall.

In actual life, however, owing to the complexity of the human heart, these two forms of danger, namely, discouragement and presumption, are not so clearly separated as we describe them above. As we shall probably have occasion to mention again, very often this feeling of weakness and fear is somewhat mixed with presumption in the fall of a soul that was truly converted and has even been fervent. Remember the denial of St. Peter. However, it is very important to distinguish the two cases in describing the dangers of temptation. We shall distinguish them by designating them under the accepted terms of: *Voluntary Temptation,* the one we seek ourselves, the one into which imprudently we want to enter; and *Spontaneous Temptation,* the one that is experienced without any connivance on our part, the one we have not sought, the one which comes to us as a pure consequence of our nature or even of our duties of state.

Temptation offers a formidable danger only under the first form, because we throw ourselves into it without the excuse of our duties of state and without the assurance of the grace of God, since we are acting expressly against His command. We should, therefore, avoid this danger at any cost; and Jesus, in His agony, begs us do so. However, also under the second form temptation constitutes a danger, if the soul that undergoes this providential trial does not understand it and lacks confidence. The soul should reassure itself that God in His merciful providence will give it the grace needed to escape the danger of temptation and to obtain from this trial the advantage of a closer union with Jesus. Let us, at this point then, listen to Jesus as He begs us to watch and pray lest we enter into the snare and hidden dangers of willful temptation. In the next chapter we shall learn, by remaining always near to Jesus how to understand and even employ unforeseen temptations in such manner as to avoid their dangers and garner their fruits. Finally, as we have already indicated, we shall speak separately of lukewarmness.

Voluntary Temptations as Jesus Saw Them

The agony in Gethsemani was for Jesus Himself a bitter crisis of temptation, temptation to push aside the chalice which the Father was presenting to Him. In this crisis from which His divine holiness could not but emerge triumphant, Jesus realized all our weaknesses in the face of temptation. What share did this vision have in the fear which crushed His heart to the breaking point and to the sweating of blood? We shall never know. We do know that He thought of our weakness, doubled by our presumption, and that He suffered on account of it. To save us from this weakness He forgot His own sorrow or rather it was His sorrow in face of the evil of sin, His sorrow for His own life attacked in our soul by mortal sin, which caused Him to endeavor to save this life by protecting us from this evil. He arose from His agonized prostration and came to us in the person of the three sleeping disciples. Thrice He came to repeat to us the dire but saving words: "Watch ye, and pray that ye enter not into temptation. The spirit indeed is willing, but the flesh weak."[3]

O Jesus, help us to understand and to heed these salutary words, by making us see that temptation is a snare into which we should never enter. Teach us to watch and pray to discover this snare and to avoid it.

"That ye enter not": Do not enter into the snare of temptation. Our Lord did not use the word "snare." But the idea is clearly contained in His words: "Watch ye, and pray that ye enter not into temptation." It is as if our Lord were telling us: "Temptation is a snare ever set, and to which you must never consent."[4] A snare, while hidden, is a very real danger. Once discovered it ceases to be a danger, because, seeing it, we seek to avoid it.

So far as we are concerned, the hidden danger lies in the ever persistent weakness of our nature which we want to forget and ignore. "The flesh is weak." The flesh indeed remains weak, the flesh by which, in the style of the New

---

[3] Mt. 26:41 ff.; Mk. 14:37.
[4] Lagrange, O.P., *L'Evangile selon saint Marc*, p. 364 f.

Testament, is meant our whole nature, body, soul, and heart: and we forget and ignore this weakness. "The spirit indeed is willing." Grace gives us zeal and fervor; yet this very zeal and fervor may serve to hide from us our poverty and weakness and render the snare even more dangerous. We feel converted, we see ourselves filled with love toward the Father and toward Jesus; for months and years we have avoided sin and persevered in this love; all this keeps us from seeing how deeply rooted the affection for sin still remains in us. In the face of temptation, this affection for sin, be it some vestige of affection toward the object of some past sin or some unlawful new inclination, will lead us to want to stop and dally, to look around for a while, and finally to enter. . . . No, we repeat to ourselves, we will not be trapped; this snare does not constitute a real danger for us. We can play with it, we can enter into it, we can even taste the bait to satisfy somewhat our liking or affection for the sin, we can do all this without any serious risk, for we feel ourselves strong and sure of stopping in time. Are we not resolved to die rather than to fall into mortal sin?

If we continue thus to enter into temptation, it will enmesh us and carry us away in its clutches. For our affection toward sin will become ever more demanding and powerful, our conscience more and more silent and blinded, and our will less stable, due to fright and anxiety and to the mesmerizing presence and attraction of evil. In a word, love for the object of the temptation, be it what it may, will gradually become so dominant in our heart that it will supplant love for God, our last end, and thus the definition of mortal sin will be verified in our soul.

All these steps are truly contained in the words of our divine Master: Do not enter into temptation. Thus far we have merely skimmed the surface of these salutary and illuminating words. Let us listen further to our Lord that we may fully

THE THREE STAGES OF THE SPIRITUAL LIFE

understand His lesson. "Watch ye, and pray that ye enter not . . . ": Watch and pray to discover and to avoid the snare of temptation. We must distinguish the two ways in which this hidden danger may appear.

First Case: The Danger May Lie in the Very Lightness of the Temptation

The temptation appears distinctly. We feel it with its evil attraction. It matters little what brought it about: our memory, our imagination, our feelings, or some external circumstance. It is really present. A doubt against faith, a thought of freedom or of pride . . . some recollection, or imagination, or curiosity, immodest and wholly inexcusable . . . the beginnings of some marks of affection that are out of place unless one has or can have marriage in view, because where the second and succeeding steps are forbidden, the first one is not permitted either. . . .

We see very well that there is some danger in all this; but the danger is so slight in itself, so far from mortal sin. . . . Moreover, we are not children any more; and again we are so sure of ourselves; we will stop whenever we want. . . . We can, therefore, without exposing ourselves to the risk of sinning mortally, dally momentarily with these doubts, these dreams of pride, these recollections, imaginations, or curiosity, these demonstrations of sensible affection. . . . We forget and ignore the words of our divine Saviour; we want to prove them wrong. He tells us not to enter; we want to enter into temptation, sure of stopping in time.

Alas, no! If we persist in entering and playing on the slippery ground of doubts against faith, of proud desires, of sentimental dreams, of rather free affections, we shall become more and more and almost fatally engulfed. "Watch and pray," Jesus pleads with us in His agony. Watch! Be on the alert to discover the snare which our attraction for sin and our presumption endeavor to hide from us. And once we discover it, let us leave at once this zone of danger and get out of the temptation. Pray! In practice vigilance brings with it prayer, or, better, vigilance identifies itself with prayer. A short but true prayer is the best protection as soon as we discover the danger. By prayer we disown, we chase away the temptation. And if it should persist, then it is no longer a voluntary temptation; it is a spontaneous one that has come and lingers in spite of us, a temptation which can help to sanctify us.

Daily experience often sadly confirms the words of our Saviour. How far back must we go to discover the first step on the fatal road which brought about a disregard for the religious life, apostasy from the faith, a sin against chastity? Back to some mere trifle, we could almost say, if we could call it a trifle to contemn the supreme plea of the suffering Saviour, if we could call a trifle the beginning of the ruination of a Christian life, a life dedicated to God. We must go back to those first willful dreams of independence, of freedom from the authority of a superior whom we did not like very well; to those dilettante poses of erudition that delight in citing and praising the works of unbelievers and in finding fault with our traditions and beliefs; to manifestations and declarations of an affection in which piety and sentimentality were mixed and which could result only in the gradual disappearance of piety and the eventual sway of sentimentality.

Second Case: The Temptation, With All Its Danger, Lies Hidden in What Appears to Be a Legitimate and Good Cause

In this second case the temptation does not present itself directly; we do not see it and do not wish it except in *its cause,* an action, some reading, certain friendships or affections that are capable in themselves of bringing on the temptation, that is, of begetting the thought and the attraction of the sin. The hidden danger of the snare consists, in this case, in the seeming harmlessness and even in the goodness and usefulness of the cause. Deceiving ourselves, we take these appearances as a pretext for entertaining the cause and in that way entering into the temptation that follows.

Before going any further, we must clarify two points to prevent any error and any scruple. In the first place, we are speaking of true causes of temptation, of readings, of actions, of relations that are truly capable of begetting in the soul the thought and the attraction of evil. There is no question whatever of merely external occasions where our subjective dispositions, our imagination, our nerves, our scrupulosity would find matter for temptation. For instance, if we go out, we shall see this or that immodest thing; if we eat this, if we drink that, we shall surely be tempted; if we speak of the love of God, even devoutly, if we read excellent books on the love of God, we shall expose ourselves to troublesome imaginations and impressions. And so forth and so on. . . . All this is purely subjective. The temptation comes from ourselves, from our nerves, from our excessive fear, and not from the cause to which we attribute it. We are not considering cases like these; we should dismiss them purely and simply.

There is question not only of true causes of temptation but also of voluntary causes, that is, causes that are in no way whatever imposed by our duties of state or by the necessities of life or by legitimate usefulness and propriety, but are truly sought and brought about by us, simply because we want them. If the cause of the temptation is imposed upon us, then this cause is in no way voluntary. This may be the case, for instance, when we have some examinations to prepare or some charitable ministry to perform; again, when there is a real necessity or usefulness, for example, a dangerous occasion which a person may find in his family relationship and he is unable to escape; also in the matter of classical studies and culture in accordance with one's social condition; again, even in accepted proprieties, such as visits or necessary acquaintance-ships. In cases such as these we may truthfully say before God and before our conscience that we do not desire the temptation in any way. We want the cause merely in view of the good result (propriety, usefulness, necessity, duties of state); we do foresee the temptations, but we find a legitimate and pro-portionate reason to suffer them in view of the good result, which is the thing that we really want.

This conception is of prime importance. It is basic in ethical science, for we are merely applying the so-called principle of the double effect, which deals with cases, so frequent in our personal and social life, when we are allowed to place a cause, although foreseeing a bad effect from it, as long as another effect, produced as immediately as — that is, not by means of — the bad one, compensates by its goodness for this latter evil. Our Lord did not have in mind these cases of temptation where the cause is truly imposed by necessity, usefulness, or propriety when He warned us not to enter into temptation. In each of these cases the temptation is allowed according to the principle of double effect. Our duty is to be humble and prudent in the face of these temptations. The grace of God will always be present to help us, since they are permitted by His will.

We come finally to the case our Lord had in mind: If the cause of the temptations is a true and voluntary cause, not one imposed upon us, but a cause sought and desired by us, then we are really in the presence of a snare, and Jesus tells us: Watch and pray that you do not enter into it. Since the cause of the temptation is in no way imposed upon us by any duty or any real advantage, then, if we seek and desire that cause we are doing it merely for the sake of the temptation itself. Our inclination toward the sin and our presumption draw us to it and seek every plausible and vain pretext the better to hide the snare from us. Thus they may suggest such pretexts as the interest of our studies, of our literary or moral training, to cause us to delve into imprudent and disturbing books of medicine, of romance, of untimely casuistry; or the need of relaxation and rest, in places where even an honest Christian should not be seen; or they may appeal to the customs of the day: "After all, everybody is reading that book, attending such a performance, following the fashion"; or to the need of affection and even of understanding help in our ministry: some conversations, it is true, some familiarities bother one's conscience somewhat but, on the other hand, we are deriving good for our soul, for the souls of others. . . . All these pretexts are deceiving. . . . It is the snare denounced by our Lord. . . . And we continue to enter into it, and let ourselves be enmeshed more and more by its deadly tentacles. . . . Is sin very far away?

There is only one means to save ourselves from sin, no matter how close we may have come to it, and that is to obey once and for all the great words of salvation: Watch and pray . . . watch to see the danger and pray for the strength to flee from it. And if we do not see the danger clearly by ourselves, for who is there who can see clearly in his own case, especially with a conscience dulled and dominated by the attraction of the sin, if we do not see the danger clearly, then we must have recourse to the guide of our soul and must tell him dutifully what is bothering and frightening us. His advice will hurt us but will save us, if we obey him when he repeats to us the words: *Do not enter,* do not dally any longer with that temptation.

There exists one last fallacy which we must avoid. A soul

dominated by the attraction of sin or by a passion or an affection may pray, but only to excuse itself from watching. Jesus asks us to pray and to watch, to make our prayer the support and the help of our vigilance. Once we recognize the danger and discover the snare, we must pray to have the strength to avoid and break any ties with it. We must not pray to have the strength to remain in the temptation and to continue our dangerous play with it, that is to say, to continue to enjoy those dangerous liberties, those dear but disturbing friendships, without running the risk of sinning mortally. Such a prayer would be immoral. It is a prayer that tempts God, for it asks Him to become our accomplice in our attraction for sin, to allow us to enjoy its taste without committing it, to throw ourselves into the flame without burning.

Unfortunately such prayers are not as rare as we think. "Father," a young working girl was telling me one Friday afternoon, "help me to make an extra good Communion tomorrow." "Why this extra good Communion?" "Well, you see, Father, my boy friend is a Protestant. I really do not intend to marry him, but I like him and he sometimes takes me to a show on Saturday nights. Sometimes, they are not very good. My conscience has bothered me; I have gone to confession. We are going out tomorrow and I want to make a good Communion so that there will be nothing wrong with the show or with him." Poor child! I did my best to make her see that she should make a good Communion to have the strength not to go to such entertainments and to break off with that boy. Did I convince her?

How many others who should know better than this young girl still pray and go to Communion, to be able to enter without danger into temptation, to enjoy certain liberties, to continue certain friendships. I have heard from someone who should have known better: "Father, I promise even to take the discipline from now on before making these visits, but do not forbid me to make them." I answered: "Leave the discipline aside, but also discontinue such visits." Did I convince him?

O Jesus, speak to us Yourself that our hearts be moved and our mind convinced. Help us to keep gratefully and forever in our soul the words of Your saving love: "Watch and pray, that ye enter not into temptation."

Chapter VIII ❧ Spontaneous Temptations,
Their Dangers and Their Benefits

THE man who has been sincerely converted to God will not
escape the attacks of temptation, even though he is careful
to watch and pray so as not to enter them voluntarily.
Temptation is a necessary law of our nature as well as a
providential trial that tests our fidelity to God. There is no
need to elaborate further upon this important truth. Let us
note that when we speak of unavoidable temptations we are
not referring merely to temptations against holy purity. The
soul newly turned to God may be attacked by temptations
against any of the virtues; and often quite strongly.

> My God, it is very hard to feel as it were identified with
> us the very evil that we detest and that we strive with all our
> will to repel. Yes, it is a frightening thing to have faith and
> to feel in our soul the disquieting impression of doubt. It is a
> frightening thing to love and to strive for a virtuous and pure
> life and to feel within us the coarse, animal, overpowering
> influence of vice! . . . It is frightening to long for detachment
> of heart and feel, whether we will it or not, the influence of
> human attachments, of natural feelings, often so unruly! To
> long to have nothing here below but Thee, to tend toward
> Thee as our one supreme good . . . and to feel the impres-
> sion of distrust that casts doubts on Thy mercy! Yes, even
> the diabolical impression of despair which can only believe,
> so it appears, in Thy hatred, in a final and irremediable
> reprobation. . . .[1]

But no matter how terrifying temptations may be in

---

[1] *Fleurs et fruits de Manreze* (Paris, 1885), p. 118.

themselves, it is God's intention that they should turn to our benefit. As the author of the *Imitation* tells us: "All the Saints passed through many tribulations and temptations and profited by them."[2] We know this and we believe it; but, unfortunately, often merely in theory. In practice we too frequently find only dangers in this trial instead of fruits of humility, of confidence, of a more intimate union with God.

I. *The Dangers of Spontaneous Temptations*

First Danger: The Risk of Falling Into a Grave Sin

Sometimes, especially if it lacks humility and confidence, the soul attacked by a purely spontaneous temptation may be astonished, then grow weary, and even be incensed against God for submitting it to such a difficult test. Are these sentiments, tainted by pride and mistrust, very far from discouragement, from haunting ideas of weakness, from the obsession of defeat, and finally from the frenzy that causes a fall? It is a fall where nerves, impressions, and physiological infirmity play a great part. It is a fall that God in His goodness will easily forgive and repair, if we approach Him with simplicity and put ourselves under His care. But it is also a grave fault; for the evil of mortal sin, even one of weakness, is very grave. To help and above all to preserve this soul from a similar danger in the future, we must first of all inspire it with deep confidence, and then instruct it on the necessity and the fruits of temptation.

Second Danger: Ruin of the Health and of the Spiritual Vitality of the Individual

How many young people who, in the seminary or in the novitiate, gave a well-founded hope of good health, of talent,

---

[2] *Imitation of Christ,* Book I, Chap. 13.

of future works, and above all of generosity, have withered, within a very short time, in body, in soul, and in heart! They became mediocre subjects all along the line. Why? Often because they did not accept, because they did not understand, that certain crises of violent and prolonged temptation to which Divine Providence submitted them, were meant to render them humbler, purer, more enlightened. And we wonder whether this was not due to the fact that at times these young people were neither sustained nor directed during such unexpected and troublesome trials.

Third and More Common Danger: Uneasiness and Annoyance With Regard to God

For some time after it has been tempted the soul seems to have the feeling "that something has come between itself and Jesus." Passing impressions of doubt seem to have clouded its faith; it feels as though evil thoughts and images are tarnishing its purity. Long ago, the author of the *Imitation* warned us against this artifice of the evil spirit who, if he is unable to stop us from receiving Communion, will endeavor by these suggestions of doubt and impurity to prevent a heart to heart union with Jesus.[3]

Last Danger: The Loss of Time in the Work of Our Perfection

How many souls who go frequently to confession lose much of the fruit of the great sacrament of penance because they devote too much time to the examination and accusation of temptations that are purely spontaneous! On this point, some confessors would tell us: We grant that the accusation of mere temptations should not take the place of the accusation

---

[3] *Imitation of Christ*, Book IV, Chap. 10.

of true deliberate venial sins. But would you not advise souls who go frequently to confession and who examine their conscience faithfully to add to the accusation of truly deliberate venial sins the accusation of temptations that are purely spontaneous? Mistakes come so easily, especially in matters of chastity. Also, is there not the priceless advantage of establishing and keeping souls in absolute security to be gained by accustoming them to accuse themselves of temptations in this matter "as God sees them guilty," even when they feel sure that they did not consent? Not to mention the grace of humility that these painful and oft-repeated accusations bring with them.

Without taking issue with these reasons, we prefer to make the following distinction: in cases where nervousness and obsession are rather rare, and where self-love can very easily insinuate and conceal itself, as, for instance, in temptations against charity and obedience or in manifestations of vanity, we would, generally speaking, allow the penitent to accuse himself of impressions and tendencies which may be purely spontaneous. Perhaps at times we would even advise it. The examination and accusation of these matters do help to improve one's self-knowledge and to increase humility. There is, also, through the reception of absolution, the great advantage of washing frequently in the Blood of the Lamb those remnants of self-love in which so often some complicity of the will lies concealed, even in instances that appear to be merely a matter of impressions. But when there is question of temptations into which nervousness and obsession can easily penetrate and play a great part, and of which ordinarily our self-love is not the direct cause — to be specific, in temptations against faith or against chastity — in these cases, we do not believe that there is any advantage but rather there may be serious inconveniences in accustoming penitents to accuse themselves of temptations that are purely spontaneous.

We are asked: in these delicate matters where mistakes come so easily should we not strive to establish and keep souls in absolute security by means of these accusations, and even by acts of perfect contrition until such souls have an opportunity to go to confession? But are we in fact offering security to souls by such means? No; on the contrary, we are upsetting them and leading them astray. For we know very well that ordinarily these prolonged and violent temptations against faith and against chastity presuppose a nervous temperament that is inclined to scrupulosity. It is unwise, under the pretext of calm and security, to recommend to such souls that they make immediately an act of perfect contrition and then accuse themselves of these temptations in their regular confession.

Silence, on the advice of the confessor, is the means best suited to bring peace and security to these souls.

Evidently, before recommending silence in regard to these temptations, the confessor will take time and care to see his way clearly. With what sort of person is he dealing? What is the point at issue? Once he sees that he is dealing with an upright, loyal, and pious soul, perhaps with a soul already advanced in perfection or at least called to advance in perfection; once he recognizes after a few confessions the tendencies and the needs of a soul that should rather be fighting selfishness than worrying over unavoidable temptations; and especially once he has asked pertinent and necessary questions and has convinced himself that this soul has not given rise to these temptations, to these dreams, to these unhealthy curiosities, to these sensible affections; then, without hesitation, let him advise silence and contempt for them. Is there anything more illogical and more enervating than to recommend acts of perfect contrition until the next regular confession? If there is guilt in these matters, it is grave. In this case, we know the general rule: Communion is forbidden until we have approached the sacrament of penance. But if there is really no guilt, then why trouble the soul and expose it to scruples by recommending conditional acts of perfect contrition? If it is handled as we suggest, the trial that torments the soul will soon cease, unless God in His inscrutable designs prolongs it. Even if the crisis lasts, the soul will feel peace and security because it will have received light and strength.

May we speak at least of a grace of humility associated with these examinations and these confessions? No, for this would be to confuse the noble and beautiful virtue of humility with fear, nervousness, and perhaps with obsession. What a disastrous formation for young religious, for the future priest, is this education gnawed by obsessions under the cover of humility! On the contrary, how many truly religious and priestly souls never bring to the confessional those useless encumbering accusations! Were we to seek for the starting point of these priceless states of conscience, we should find it in the judicious formation they received in the novitiate or in the seminary, which gave these loyal and watchful souls strength never to enter into voluntary temptations and rendered them so discerning, calm, humble, and confident that they treat with silence and contempt all spontaneous temptations.

Even if there were no danger of nervousness and obsession in these examinations and these accusations, they would, nevertheless, be too often the cause of losing in part the fruits of the sacrament of penance which we mentioned above. There would be a loss of time in the general work of perfection. Who has not known those pious souls in the world, those religious and priestly souls also, who without going as far as scruples and obsession, wear themselves out in a useless fight against spontaneous temptations, and, as a result, lack the attention and energy needed to watch and fight against their dominant fault, the deep-rooted source of an egoism that causes so many flights of temper, so many criticisms, such a painful and unedifying pettiness? Their dominant fault has full rein because their spiritual strength is absorbed and exhausted in the fight against the illusions of spontaneous temptations; and this may have been going on for years! What a peaceful revelation, what an interior transformation awaits these souls when finally seeing their mistake they abandon this tiring and troublesome struggle against spontaneous temptations and direct their efforts against their self-love!

II. *The Benefits of Spontaneous Temptations*

If we were writing directly for priests, we should attempt to fathom the mystery of the sacerdotal temptation of Jesus, as St. Paul reveals it to us:

> and so he must needs become altogether like his brethren; he would be a high priest who could feel for us and be our true representative before God. . . . It is because he himself has been tried by suffering, that he has power to help us in the trials we undergo.[4]
>
> It is not as if our high priest was incapable of feeling for us in our humiliations; he has been through every trial, fashioned as we are, only sinless.[5]

And we should find that for us priests, as for Jesus Christ, the Priest thrice Holy, temptations should be a source of intelligent and merciful compassion toward unfortunate souls, "who could feel for us"; of valiant supplication in our prayer for the Christian people, "our true representative before God"; a great means of expiating with Jesus, "to make atonement for the sins of the people."

---

[4] Hebr. 2:17 f.
[5] Cf. Hebr. 4:15.

Let us remain, however, in the field of the purgative way and see how in designs of Divine Providence, who allows it, the trial of spontaneous temptation should unite our soul more intimately with Jesus, our Saviour:

By teaching us to pray in His name with humility and confidence,

By teaching us to share in the strength and beauty of His own virtue,

By teaching us to share in the very mystery of His atoning temptation.

Spontaneous Temptations Should Teach Us to Pray in the Name of Jesus With Humility and Confidence

"Out of the depths have I cried to Thee." Perhaps grace has preserved us in the past from mortal sin. In any case, we remain exposed to forget that our incurable human weakness remains, despite our conversion and our good resolves to remain attached forever to God. Temptation, like the lightning that tears asunder the darkness of the night and shows us the abyss into which one more step would have plunged us — temptation makes us fathom the frightening misery where we could founder at any moment, if God's grace did not protect us against allurements and folly. There is no need actually to have fallen into the abyss to pray fervently to our Saviour. The terrifying vision of our misery suffices to draw forth the cry of distress which is a true prayer, the only true prayer, calling on the Infinite Mercy to help an almost infinite misery.

True humility exists only with confidence. It makes us see our misery in the light of God and of Jesus. The same enlightening grace that causes us to search thoroughly and to feel our misery, elevates us by this very means to the realization of the love and the help of God in Jesus. Also, it is the same enlightening grace which inspires us with the comforting and strong conviction that we are not alone the one who is attacked, but Jesus Himself in us. By threatening the life of grace in our soul, by attacking those marvels of pardon and sanctification that caused our conversion, temptation attacks the very life of Jesus in us: "And I live, now not I, but Christ liveth in me."[6] Confidence, therefore, for we are not alone the one who is praying in the temptation; it is Jesus who prays in us and for Himself.

Spontaneous Temptations Should Teach Us to Share More Fully in the Strength and Beauty of the Virtue of Jesus

Virtue implies strength, and strength is developed by exercise. In baptism we receive many virtues, but they are only dispositions and powers of action; they are not in act. Virtue, in order to become active and grow, needs exercise and struggle. Temptations offer to our virtue one of the best providential opportunities to exercise itself and to struggle. The increase in strength and beauty which virtue acquires in its struggle against temptation is well explained by the following comparisons.

The soul of a child is beautiful in its baptismal innocence; it is a soul whiter than the swaddling clothes that cover the tiny body; it is a soul admired by the angels and pleasing to God. Nevertheless, this innocence, unacquainted with struggle, is more the absence of any stain than positive purity. Even supposing grace and virtues, the life of Jesus, in that soul, we can truly say that such innocence, which up to now has not struggled, is only the absence of stain, although it possesses in potency a very rich reserve of active and hard-won purity. Temptation will supply material for the exercise and development of this potency. Thus will be produced the most

---
[6] Gal. 2:20.

beautiful sight that we are privileged to contemplate, a young man who is pure, who has punished his body to keep it in subjection, who has fought and suffered to preserve his heart for the only love worthy of him and acceptable before God.

The faith of simple and illiterate souls is beautiful; some envy it, viewing it as the expansion of the grace of baptism, undisturbed and untarnished by doubts. But how much more beautiful, radiant, and enviable is the faith of a perseveringly humble and loyal soul, who has been submitted by God to the excruciating trial of doubt; who in the midst of those tortures has humbled itself and prayed all the more; who has finally overcome the doubt by study and with help from above; who has touched, so to speak, the immovable rock whereon our certitude rests, and has lived again the experiences that are indisputable testimony to the dogma of life! How much more excellent and fruitful is this faith than the proverbial "simple faith of a poor washerwoman."

A book of meditations already quoted expresses very strikingly the same idea:

> Under the most violent attacks of unhealthy impressions, I can remain pure if I want to do so; as the rays of the sun remain pure even though they fall on sordid mire; as Thou my God, remainest pure in the most criminal soul where Thou dwellest by Thy immensity. Also, if I want it, these impressions will not only fail to stain my soul but they will purify it all the more. I will never prove myself a stronger believer than when I cling to faith in spite of impressions of doubt; I will never be more virtuous than when I give myself heart and soul to well-doing in spite of impressions of evil. For, then, it will not only be virtue, but the martyrdom of virtue; it will be the merits of fidelity joined to the merits of struggle: the crown of the just and the palm of the confessor. I promise it, therefore. Henceforward I will despise all sensible impressions of temptation; I will notice them only to humble myself before Thee, O my God, and to thank Thee. To humble myself

for all the evil that I feel within me; to thank Thee, because Thou hast cleansed me from this evil.[7]

These considerations have led us rather high. Yet we can discern a still higher plane. We have referred to it very frequently, because it is the great dogma of our faith, the dogma of our life as members of Christ, of our incorporation to Christ. Our life of grace and of virtue is undoubtedly ours; it is our treasure, the source of our holiness, the beginning of our glory. But it belongs also to Christ, who develops and consummates in each of us as members of His Mystical Body the life that fills His soul. We have also mentioned that temptation attacks the life of Christ in us. Consequently, we will preserve this life not only by praying in the name of Jesus, and by asking Him to pray for us and for His life in us, but also by sharing His own virtue, as it were, that is tempted in us and by begging Him to be more and more our light, our strength, our charity, our obedience. By reason of the temptation itself we can say: we are crucified with Christ, yet we are alive; or rather not we; it is the light, the charity, the obedience, the purity of Christ that live in us.

Spontaneous Temptations Should Teach Us to Share in the Mystery of the Atoning Temptation of Christ

Immediately before the great temptation that constituted His agony, Jesus said to Peter, John, and James, the three chosen disciples: "Stay you here, and watch with me."[8] He was asking them to share in His agony, in His momentous atoning temptation. It was a singular invitation. But they did not understand Him and they failed Him: "He found them sleeping, for sorrow."[9] Jesus asks us the same thing.

---

[7] *Fleurs et fruits de Manreze*, p. 118 f.
[8] Mt. 26:38.
[9] Lk. 22:45; Mk. 14:40.

Would that we might understand the mystery of His atoning temptation, and the necessity as well as the honor of being associated with it.

The Christian soul, it seems, does not like to contemplate the mystery of the tempted Saviour. Jesus on that occasion descends too low, far lower than at Bethlehem and on the cross. The mystery of a God-Man, even of a dying God-Man, is above us, but we do not find it repugnant. Before the mystery of the temptation of Jesus, however, we may experience something like moral aversion. The Being of Light, deigning to lend even an attentive ear to the suggestions of the spirit of darkness; the Being of all holiness, undergoing, feeling the contact of the being of corruption; no, never has Jesus descended so low! But He did suffer this supreme humiliation and He accepts it before the holiness and love of His Father in expiation and reparation for sin.

Because sin continues in this world, the atoning temptation of Christ must also continue: "to make atonement for the sins of the people." But since Jesus is now unable to suffer Himself, He will suffer in the members of His Mystical Body. Hence the converted soul, feeling still the nearness of its sinful past life, should also feel the pressing need and duty to pray and to make reparation with Jesus; it should be ready to share more intimately in the mystery of the temptation of the Saviour. It would seem as if the person who would fathom this mystery would be almost irresistibly led to ask God to submit him to the trial of temptation. Yet, our weakness will never utter such a prayer. But if God deigns to call us to share in this supreme expiation of Jesus, our heart will also share in His *Fiat* so grateful and yet so forlorn.

Chapter IX ❧ Lukewarmness, Another Obstacle to Lasting Conversion

As WE have already said, the converted soul can return and fall into mortal sin more surely and more fatally by lukewarmness or tepidity, than by voluntary entrance into temptation. More than dangerous playing with temptation, which can be accidental and can be easily repaired, lukewarmness ruins basically the work of true conversion since it supposes and brings with it the decay of the entire spiritual organism. It is important, therefore, to study its true nature; to discover the influence and the tendencies that favor its growth; to follow its fatal march toward the abyss, that is toward mortal sin, the result of slow spiritual decay; and, finally, to learn the remedy which can cure us of this evil and especially the means which can preserve us forever from it.

I. The True Nature of Lukewarmness

Many pious and devout souls are frightened by this word, *lukewarmness*. They mistake it for a synonym of spiritual aridity or the habitual lack of sensible consolation in the performance of their spiritual exercises and their duties of state. This thought grieves and frightens them. Aridity and disgust can well be a sign or a result of lukewarmness; but, in order to conclude to the existence of lukewarmness, we need other indications besides the simple fact of aridity or of disgust, because, frequently enough, total lack of religious feeling exists hand in hand with a real and solid piety.

For this reason, some authors prefer to distinguish between lukewarmness of feeling and lukewarmness of will. It is better perhaps to limit this name to the lukewarmness of the will, which is the only true one. Father Desurmont describes it in this manner:

> To be lukewarm, obstinately so, means to have made a pact with certain venial sins on the one hand, and with God on the other. It means to say to sin: I am keeping you and I have no desire to live without you! It means to say to God: Although I want to continue sinning, I still want to remain Your friend. . . . If in the secrecy of my free-will I divide myself equally between good and evil; if I reject mortal sin because it will destroy my soul, but accept venial sin because it is only venial, I am keeping both heat and cold within myself. . . . I am lukewarm.[1]

Perhaps this psychological analysis is more explicit and more dramatized than what we find in reality. For in lukewarmness there is only one movement, that of attachment to venial sin, even though it carries with it a more or less vague desire to keep God's friendship by avoiding mortal sin. Hence spiritual writers agree in defining lukewarmness as the state of a soul which sacrifices habitually the love of God to the love of self on some point which is not in itself matter for mortal sin, but which nevertheless offers some danger. This is the definition proposed by Father LeGaudier: "Lukewarmness in charity is self-love habitually preferred to love for God on some point not mortal but dangerous." Others present it more concretely. Dom Chautard says: "To be lukewarm means to make a covenant with dissipation and carelessness, habitually yielded to or not resisted, a covenant with deliberate venial sin." Desurmont puts it very simply: "Lukewarmness means to have taken sides with deliberate venial sin."[2]

---

[1] Desurmont, C.SS.R., *L'art d'assurer son salut*, pp. 205–210.

[2] LeGaudier, *op. cit.*, I, 244. Dom Chautard, *The Soul of the Apostolate*, p. 77 f. (trans. by J. A. Moran, S.M., Techny, 1943). Desurmont, *op. cit*; also *Le retour continuel a Dieu*, p. 47 f.

Perhaps some concrete examples will be better than these abstract descriptions and definitions, because they will help us to see better how lukewarmness exists in the converted soul, in a soul vowed to perfection.

A soul is lukewarm which lets itself be dominated by love of ease and horror of sacrifice, and comes, as a consequence, to omit any painful duty that is not imposed *sub gravi,* to turn against inevitable crosses, against any discomfort; to be, almost unconsciously, badly disposed toward authority both human and divine.

A soul is lukewarm which little by little has acquired and maintains an attitude of antipathy toward some of its companions, or a discontented and critical attitude toward the authority of its superiors.

A soul is lukewarm which yields, moved mostly by natural inclinations, to friendships which will result in continual preoccupations, jealousies, indiscreet confidences, and unbecoming proofs of affection.

A soul is lukewarm which through curiosity, frivolity, pride, and an unhealthy taste for rationalistic or sentimental literature, reads any kind of book, attends any sort of play, just as if the rules of prudence, modesty, humility, and faith were not meant for it.

These are only a few cases. Even they are still very far from reality. It is so hard to grasp and to describe thoroughly the innermost recesses of a soul, especially when the soul itself is more or less unconscious of the depth of the self-love that dominates its impressions and even, in a certain sense, its most deliberate decisions. This occurs particularly in those cases of lukewarmness in which the soul is blinded and baffled by the influence of its self-love, that is to say, by its incurable affection for sin. Therefore, if we desire that our descriptions come closer to reality, we must bring out this point about delusion in the cases we presented, since this delusion is, to a degree, both unconscious and imputable.

Let us recall the general delusion of the lukewarm soul: it believes itself determined to avoid mortal sin at any cost and feels sure that it will avoid it. Let us remember also that each particular case paints and hides itself in the colors and shades of the individual egotism as it searches for pretexts and excuses.

The person dominated by love of ease, who avoids sacrifice and discomfort, finds an excuse in his delicate health, in the amount of work that he is already doing, in the past services that he has rendered, and also in the selfishness of others who are not working as hard as he.

The person who seeks sensible affections will say that his nature is made in that way, that he must have some compensation for the sacrifice he made of family joys, that his intention is right, pure, and zealous: he is merely seeking help and sympathy in the work that he is doing; he has done much good to the persons with whom he associates. . . . Moreover, others do the same thing.

The person who nourishes antipathy and the spirit of criticism will say with a certain amount of sincerity: "I treat my companions as they treat me. I am defending myself. Besides, the authorities are prejudiced and unjust toward me, they show too much favoritism."

Finally, the person who imprudently reads any book or attends any play, will plead the need of relaxation, especially during vacation time; he will appeal to a need for intellectual or artistic culture, to the duty of being "up to date," to the fact that the "better" class of people read and see these things.

There, in those delusions, lies hidden the real danger; there we find the symptoms of this dreadful malady: "This disease is the more harmful inasmuch as, generally, it breaks out stealthily under innocuous appearances."[3]

---

[3] LeGaudier, *op. cit.,* p. 246.

II. Tendencies and Influences That Favor the Growth of Lukewarmness

If a person that has been converted lets himself be over-taken and dominated by lukewarmness, it is always through his own fault. He has grown lax in prayer and in the struggle against the dominant self-love which attracts him to sin. Lukewarmness is always the result of a weakening of the will. This weakening of the will is due in part to various interior predispositions and exterior influences.

Predispositions to Lukewarmness

1. A Rather Active Temperament That Devotes Itself to External Works Without the Counterbalance of Prayer

The theme is a classical one since the book *De consideratione*, which St. Bernard addressed to a pope who seemed over-occupied with external affairs, down to *The Soul of the Apostolate*, which Dom Chautard wrote for the priests of our own days who are under the terrific pressure of unrelenting demands of the active ministry. Human nature feels little attraction for piety. Of itself it tends rather to action. True or imaginary success will only augment this feverish activity; spiritual exercises will be shortened or even abandoned alto-gether, especially those that are not strictly imposed by the law of God or of the Church; those that are retained will be performed at the last minute, in a hurry, all at once, with no more care and attention than if they were merely a material obligation. Is it any wonder that impressions and evil influences regain their hold on a life that is wanting in direction and interior strength?[4]

2. A Weak Constitution, a Melancholic Temperament

Worries about his health, the anticipation and fear of

---

[4] Chautard, *op. cit.*, pp. 77–90; LeGaudier, *op. cit.*, I, 181 ff., 213 ff.

future trials, the exaggeration of his own deficiencies, failings, and blunders, cause a young man to be discouraged and saddened and lead him to an early pessimism and cause him to abandon the only two forces that keep the soul away from sin, namely, prayer and vigilance.

3. *A Mind That Perceives Too Keenly the Weaknesses of Human Nature, Unless Its View Be Transformed by Piety and Charity*

Discernment and perspicacity are priceless possessions, but they must be accompanied by other qualities as well as by other virtues. Without supernatural motivation, without piety and humility, without kindness and charity, we shall see only the defects and miseries around us. Certain contacts, certain experiences will perhaps reveal to us weaknesses in places where we should never have suspected them. From these arise surprise, scandal, premature skepticism, slanderous generalizations, painful observations with regard to particular individuals, and, above all, a disheartening inclination to abandon all efforts, which offers as an excuse our so-called verifications of a universal egotism.

Exterior Influences That Favor Lukewarmness

We shall call attention here only to the unedifying examples that very often are present when laxness begins. Some revered person, a man of apparently "good common sense," who in the past has been devoted to his work, will make fun of the strict formation in seminaries or in the novitiate, will lower the priestly or the religious ideal, will speak of a needed adaptation of old rules to the new times and places; and without realizing it, he will perhaps prepare the downfall of his younger companion, who has been fervent but who now by reason of the words and example of this person whom he esteems is led little by little to carelessness and tepidity.[5]

III. The Fatal March Toward the Abyss, That Is, Toward Mortal Sin, the Result of Slow Spiritual Decay

Let us keep in mind that we are speaking here of a decision taken to spare and to satisfy one's self-love, of a pact made with venial sin on some point which of itself is not matter of mortal sin but which nevertheless offers some danger: "on some point not mortal but dangerous," as Father LeGaudier expresses it; some point, for instance, that touches more or less directly on the delicate ground of obedience, chastity, faith, charity.

Negligence concerning venial sin on secondary points, for example, some small attachment to worldly goods, some gluttony mixed perhaps with the vanity of posing as a connoisseur of good wines and good cheer, some boastful mannerisms affected while singing, preaching, or even in sports, in order to impress people; negligence on these points or similar ones will constitute an obstacle to perfection, will diminish considerably the efficacy of our zeal, may cause us much distress and pain; but in itself, it offers no danger of leading to lukewarmness.

We shall remain, then, in the clear-cut field of true lukewarmness. However, in order to make our analysis more precise and clear, we shall distinguish in this march toward mortal sin, which is only one movement, these two features: the gradual weakening of spiritual energies and the parallel growing power of evil tendencies.

The Gradual Weakening of Spiritual Energies

In practice it comes down to the weakening of the spirit of

---

[5] LeGaudier, *op. cit.,* p. 192 f.

faith by the atrophy of the spirit or life of prayer. The lukewarm soul wants to satisfy its self-love at the expense of the
love of God on some rather important point. How often
this self-love will cause it to give up spiritual exercises that are
not absolutely obligatory? In the disposition in which that soul
finds itself, will it be able in reality to pray? True prayer is
"an elevation of the mind and heart to God," "a cordial conversation with our Heavenly Father," "communion to the
life of loving adoration and intercession of Jesus." No matter
what definition we choose, we can see that refusal to sacrifice
ourselves on some vital point creates a sort of constraint or
uneasiness in our relations with God, something incompatible
with true prayer. Without going to extremes, we must admit
at least that the person who is, and wants to remain, attached
to his self-love, cannot at the same time raise his spirit to
his Heavenly Father and engage in filial conversation with
Him in the aura of the love of Jesus.

Yet, without prayer, without true prayer, there is no spirit,
no life of faith. Prayer, whether of adoration or of petition,
passes into act, that is to say, obtains for us and brings us
grace, the force of light and love, the principle of our supernatural life and action. In the measure that true prayer
diminishes in a soul, in the same degree will the grace of light
and love diminish. The life of that soul is invaded and
overrun by natural and selfish impressions, by its dominant
self-love. It savors "not the things that are of God, but the
things that are of men."[6] This brings us to the second element
of our analysis.

The Growing Power of Evil Tendencies

Day by day, these tendencies become more and more tyran-
nical and exacting. Day by day, conscience blinds itself and

---

[6] Mt. 16:23. Cf. LeGaudier, *op. cit.*, pp. 248–252.

becomes warped by vain excuses and selfish reasonings. Day by day, our will allows itself to be caught and squeezed by their ever spreading tentacles. Gradually it loses the fear and almost the feeling of sin; it loses also the power to resist the evil which it yet perceives.

Has not this soul crossed the line that separates venial from mortal sin? The soul is in doubt. Perhaps it is tempted to seek light by looking through the books of moral theology. This would be the worst way to seek enlightenment. Moralists see and judge in the abstract. Moreover, no matter how disinterested and learned they may be, they hesitate quite often to commit themselves. What help can they give to that poor soul whose conscience is half-blinded by the passions that are driving it? It will merely find in those books what it wants to find, futile new reasons to be calm while allowing the ravages of spiritual disintegration to continue. How often sin has already been committed before God, while the soul still hesitates or even refuses to admit it!

St. Thomas warned us long ago that want of fortitude in the face of hardships and horror of sacrifice produce in us a state of sorrow which breaks our spirit to such a degree that we remain hardly real men, let alone Christians: "that the mind be not broken by sorrow, and fall away from its greatness,"[7] a state of sadness which begets bitterness and rancor even against God, which ends by leading us to forbidden pleasures: "No one can long dwell in sorrow without pleasure. . . . those who find no joy in spiritual pleasures, have recourse to pleasures of the body."[8]

We have seen antipathies against a companion, attitudes of revolt against a superior end sometimes in outbursts of slander and even of calumny, in remarks subversive of authority, where there was certainly grave matter. If we may like to

[7] St. Thomas, *Summa theol.*, IIa IIae, q. 128, a. 1.
[8] St. Thomas, *Summa theol.*, IIa IIae, q. 35, a. 4, ad 2.

believe that at the moment the material fault was committed there was lack of full advertence, due to the state of nerves and of passion, we cannot say this in each case of the entire process that led to the fault. There was a time when the soul could and should have foreseen the present results. It did not want then to watch and conquer itself, although it foresaw the fatal consequence of today. It was then that it incurred before God the responsibility for its sin. Certain sensible affections willfully entertained, dangerous liberties and familiarities that a person persists in excusing despite the protests of conscience, these may have caused before God the loss of chastity, long before the actual fault was committed which finally opened the person's eyes, without being able perhaps to detach his heart from the clutches of the sin. We have known of shipwrecks in virtue and in faith due to a presumptuous curiosity that sought to read and see everything.

Such is the converted soul that has fallen back into mortal sin, a mortal sin that presupposes and completes a slow disintegration of conscience and of the entire spiritual life.[9] Undoubtedly, a return to true conversion is always possible. The mercy of God who never abandons the sinner here below will continue to make efforts to save him. It is Jansenistic to hold that the measure of graces that God destines for us can be totally exhausted years before death. No, the grace of conversion will not be lacking as long as we live. But how difficult it is for the lukewarm soul to hope and to dare to wish to return to the Father!

IV. The Remedy Which Can Cure Us and the Means Which Will Preserve Us Forever From Lukewarmness

The remedy which alone can cure us of this evil of tepidity

---

[9] Desurmont, *La volonté de se sauver en saint*, pp. 16–26.

is simply this: to begin over again the work of true conversion, to retrace step by step the purgative way, to become once again a child, a "beginner," no matter what our age may be, no matter what dignities or what knowledge we may have acquired:

> All these, if they wish to provide for their own well-being, must, even after long years and considerable success in the spiritual life, return to the starting-point and in some way begin their career anew, building the temple of spiritual perfection from its foundation.[10]

All this with great confidence, for the Divine Mercy that calls us will be constantly with us to help us.

Despite variety in presentation, all spiritual masters are unanimous in giving us as the infallible means to preserve ourselves from lukewarmness the loyalty or good will to pray and to fight all our lives.

To Pray: To pray in the measure imposed on all Christian souls by the laws of God and of the Church and by one's own director; to pray in the measure imposed on all religious and priestly souls by the holy rules of their state of life. We shall add, with regard to the Christian soul and especially the consecrated soul, the effort to pray each day more in communion with the prayer of our Lord, that is to say, in communion with His true life of loving adoration and intercession. Such a prayer surely is a guarantee of perseverance and a source of sanctification.

To Fight: We should endeavor to hear and to apply to ourselves the words of Christ: "If any man will come after me [will persevere in the state of grace and rise still higher] let him deny himself, and take up his cross, and follow me."[11]

---

[10] LeGaudier, *op. cit.,* P. II, Sect. I, Chap. III, p. 180 f., and Chap. V, pp. 191–193.

[11] Mt. 16:24.

To deny ourselves means to deny our dominant self-love, our sinful selfishness; so, there is nothing more directly opposed to lukewarmness than this fight for renunciation, since lukewarmness means to be on the side of self, on the side of our self-love.

Is not this lifelong fight in union with Jesus, associated with Him in every encounter, the way to true sanctity? It is, indeed, but the Christian, and, above all, the religious and the priest who does not want to save himself as a saint, does not really want to save himself at all.[12]

---

[12] Desurmont, *op. cit.*, pp. 25–36; LeGaudier, *op. cit.*, pp. 243–259.

Chapter X ❧ Conclusion:

Meeting With Jesus, Our Saviour

WE MENTIONED in the introduction that the dogma of our incorporation with Christ Jesus should serve to light up each step along the purgative way. Throughout these pages, we have endeavored to recall with joy, again and again, this dogma of light and life. At the end of the way, we feel that this life-giving light will lead us still higher, much higher, to the summit of the illuminative and unitive ways. Now, before continuing our ascent, we want to pause an instant to see once more how Jesus is the center, the soul of our conversion.

True conversion, as we have often said, supposes the realization of the evil of mortal sin, the evil of God, the desire to cleanse ourselves from it and to atone ever more for it, the resolution to avoid it at all cost in the future. We shall not attain this stage on our journey until we have finally met Jesus, our Saviour: Jesus, our Saviour on the cross, showing us vividly the rights and the love of the Father and the malice of mortal sin; Jesus, our Saviour in the great sacrament of penance covering our past sins with the pardon and the reparation of His precious blood; Jesus, our Saviour in the Holy Eucharist where He renews His sacrifice for our sins and gives Himself to us as the Bread of Life in the degree that He incorporates us, with our selfishness and our covetousness, to His own immolation.

Jesus, Our Saviour on the Cross

Only on Calvary, in the presence of the cross, can we fully realize God's goodness toward us and the evil of our sin toward Him. The goodness of the Father radiates in the gift of Jesus, the gift of Jesus right to the cross itself:

> And as Moses lifted up the serpent in the desert, so must the Son of man be lifted up: that whosoever believeth in him may not perish, but may have life everlasting. For God so loved the world, as to give his only-begotten Son; that whosoever believeth in him, may not perish but may have life everlasting.[1]
>
> He . . . spared not even his own Son, but delivered him up for us all, how hath he not also, with him, given us all things![2]

We see the evil of sin, evil against God in the ingratitude and the aversion of His chosen people (a figure of our soul) condemning the God-Man to death; we see this evil in the death upon the cross of the divine Victim, the only One capable of satisfying in strict justice the rights of an offended God.

Would that we might learn to meditate upon and contemplate Thy cross, O Jesus. When will we finally embrace it with all our heart and become attached to Thee alone, our Saviour: *O crux, Ave, spes unica!*

Jesus, Our Saviour in the Great Sacrament of Penance

Paul Bourget in *Un Divorce* makes an unbeliever speak thus of the reconciliation of a libertine with God through a death-bed absolution:

> Let us admit a judgment after death. . . . This judgment, in order to be just, must bear upon one's whole existence. How can it be modified by the gestures and the words of a cleric over a half-dead person, who has scarcely knowledge to think or breath to speak? And the person who answers him in the name of faith replies: "It is sufficient that he be able to

---

[1] Jn. 3:14 ff.
[2] Rom. 8:32.

repent and to unite himself in his sacrifice to the merits of the Saviour. The entire Christian faith rests on this ransom by the sufferings of the God-Man for us poor sinners. The gestures and words of the priest are only the medium of the sacrament. . . . How can you but admire, even if you do not believe in it, . . . this kindness from on high, always ready to pardon whatever we have done, provided we ask for it in the name of that Just Man, who wanted to die that we might live, for we live only through Him!"

"We live only by our conscience," interrupts the unbeliever. . . . "This Saviour is a substitute victim: a dogma of injustice, if there was ever one."

"No," replies the believer more passionately, "It is a dogma of love, of infinite love!"

This dogma of love began its action on Calvary itself, when the good thief confessed his crime, " . . . we receive the due reward of our deeds." This confession united his death with the death of the Just One. It stimulated in him the assurance of pardon and the hope of heaven: "Lord, remember me when thou shalt come into thy kingdom."[3]

We, too, must enter into this dogma of love and feel within us the power of the cross. The crucifix alone is not sufficient. It is the image, the representation of the great act of salvation; but we need to feel the precious blood fall on our sins to pardon and cleanse us; we need the great sacrament of penance. In each one of our confessions we will see and feel the power of this blood as it forgives, cleanses, and atones for our iniquities, just as we saw and felt it in the general confession of the purgative retreat. We will always approach this great sacrament as a personal meeting with our Saviour. At each confession we will place at the foot of the cross all our past sins and all the sorrowful details of our present life with their cause, our dominant selfishness. What a

---

[3] Lk. 23:40–43.

guarantee of perseverance and progress would our confessions be, if we should always approach them in this spirit!

Jesus, Our Saviour in the Eucharist

The host and the chalice are more than just a souvenir of the cross, more than the power of the cross. They are the cross itself, the sacrifice of the Body and Blood of Jesus, renewed for us, to complete and to strengthen in us the work of conversion. In the Holy Eucharist Jesus offers Himself for us each day as the Victim of expiation for our sins. He gives Himself to us as the Bread that makes us live by immolating more and more the selfishness which lies at the bottom of all our faults.

"This is my body, which is given for you."[4] "For this is my blood of the new testament, which shall be shed for many, unto remission of sins."[5] In clear and precise terms, You tell us, O Saviour, that on the eucharistic altar Your Body and Blood are offered in mystical immolation for our innumerable sins, offenses, and negligences. Our sins, so to speak, give us the place and right to be at the altar. They are, as it were, our personal contribution to the altar. From the *Confiteor* to the *Domine, non sum dignus,* everything reminds us of our iniquities. Would that we might finally see You on the eucharistic altar, and learn to avail ourselves of You, O Jesus, the expiatory Host for our sins, the Host of our salvation!

You are truly our Saviour, O Jesus. You are not satisfied to become the "Host for Sin." You become also the Bread that gives us life, by mortifying in us selfishness and concupiscence, the root of all our sins. Holy Communion should make us one with You, one with You as the Host of Love. But to become united to You, O Jesus, we must immolate more and more each day that self-love which is the great and

---

[4] Lk. 22:19.
[5] Mt. 26:28.

only obstacle to Your love. Holy Communion should make us live more in You, living as You live, for the Father: "As the living Father hath sent me, and I live by the Father; so he that eateth me, the same shall also live by me."[6] But to live Your life, O Jesus, we must renounce our life, so full of selfishness, impressions, and sins.

The more we renounce and immolate ourselves, the more we shall live in You by true conversion, the more we shall progress along the illuminative way and in the union of love. For it will no longer be we who live, but You, O Jesus, who will live in us, unto the plenitude of the perfect man.

[6] Jn. 6:58.